The Art of
Mindful Walking

The Art of
Mindful Walking

Meditations on the Path

Adam Ford

Leaping Hare Press

First published in the UK in 2011 by
Leaping Hare Press

210 High Street, Lewes
East Sussex BN7 2NS, UK
www.leapingharepress.co.uk

Text copyright © Adam Ford 2011
Design and layout copyright © The Ivy Press 2011

British Library Cataloguing-in-Publication Data
A catalogue record for this book is available from
the British Library

ISBN: 978-1-907332-58-6

This book was conceived, designed and produced by
Leaping Hare Press

Creative Director PETER BRIDGEWATER
Publisher JASON HOOK
Art Director WAYNE BLADES
Senior Editor JAYNE ANSELL
Designer RICHARD CONSTABLE
Illustrator CLIFFORD HARPER

Printed in China
Colour Origination by Ivy Press Reprographics

10 9 8 7 6 5

CONTENTS

INTRODUCTION

The first rule, if one has to have rules,
would be: 'Don't set out to do some thoughtful
walking. Just walk.' This is the great simplicity of
mindfulness as taught by the Buddha. 'When walking,
walk; when standing, stand; when sitting, sit; when
lying down, lie down.' We can make life too complicated
in our frantic effort to understand who we are
and where we have come from.

ON BEING A HUMAN

It is not easy being a human; each of us a creature with an unbroken billion-year ancestry; unique, created by God through the miraculous process of evolution, shaped by the laws of physics, chemistry and biology, and the selective pressures of the environment; a thinking, breathing, sometimes difficult, member of the rich ecosystem of our home planet.

WE DIDN'T ASK TO BE HERE and are perplexed, perhaps, about whether we have a purpose and what it might be. Our feelings and urges can make a mockery of us. We lose our poise. But 'Thought' has emerged on Earth and leapt to a new level in us – giving us a burden and a joy.

The association of thinking with walking has a long and noble history, emerging into written records with the peripatetic philosophers of ancient Greece. It is so natural to link the two that we can imagine our oldest human ancestors trudging home from the hunt, retelling the success in their minds, turning it into a story; or pondering the failure, anguishing over the loss of a favourite flint or arrowhead.

We are bodies with minds – or, if you prefer, embodied minds, depending on whether you make the body the primary reality, or you feel compelled to give priority to the mind. Either way, we are forced to live with a certain tension between the two. It is in living (and walking) with this body-

mind relationship that we begin to define who we are. There can be something spiritual about the simple physical activity of walking; it lies deep in the psyche of many religions. The psalmist in the Bible praises the person who walks in the way of God, and the earliest Christian community, taking up the idea, called themselves not Christians, but 'Followers of the Way'. The oldest religion in China, Taoism, is named after the Tao, the Way, the mysterious 'Something' that was there in the beginning before the world; it guides us back to our roots and celebrates walking in old paths. For Buddhists, the Right way of living is to follow the Eightfold Path.

What is 'Mindful Walking'?

'Mindfulness' is a lovely word, one of the great contributions made by Buddhism to the world of thinking. Mindfulness does not always come naturally to humans but has to be learnt and practised. It is part of the 'waking up' process that is the opportunity life offers to us all. The Buddha summarized his teaching in the Noble Eightfold Path – eight aspects of life that need urgent attention if we are to get anywhere in our journey towards understanding and peace. Mindfulness, *samma sati*, is the seventh element of the path, suggesting the need for attentiveness, alertness and awareness.

Walpola Rahula, renowned Buddhist scholar-monk from Sri Lanka, defines 'Right Mindfulness' in his *What the Buddha Taught* as 'attentiveness – which is to be diligently aware,

mindful and attentive with regard to (1) the activities of the body, (2) sensations or feelings, (3) the activities of the mind and (4) ideas thoughts and conceptions'. This is an essential practice if one is to avoid the sluggish temptation to sleepwalk through life. Waking up becomes an adventure. And mindfulness goes well with walking.

One of my favourite images of the Buddha is of him gently touching the earth. He sits calmly in the lotus position, one relaxed hand trailing over his crossed legs, fingertips in contact with the ground. It is known as 'the Earth-touching mode'. It refers, in the Pali tradition, to a vow he was reputed to have made in a previous life, calling the Earth as a witness, that he would one day achieve enlightenment. I see something more in it. The Buddha, while meditating, is not escaping the real world to float in some spiritual, religious realm detached from physical things. Whatever truth he finds through meditation and contemplation is rooted in the real; the spiritual and the physical are part and parcel of the same thing. The spiritual is not, as some religious types seem to imagine, a way of escape from the turmoil of the flesh.

Why Walk?

In the following chapters I shall explore the activity of walking as an exercise of body and mind, both serious and light-hearted. I will describe some walks I have done, and, by practising mindfulness, my investigation both of the reality

around me and the reality within – the feelings, thoughts, ideas and beliefs that make up the (sometimes clouded) landscape of my inner life. I grew up in a happy Christian household, my father a country parson. Later I found my way, through an interest in science (particularly astronomy) to being ordained an Anglican priest; was a vicar in West Yorkshire, a school chaplain in London and, for a time, a Priest-in-Ordinary at the Chapel Royal. I remain rooted in the Christian tradition, but with questions and often feeling an urge to move on. Some of my Christian beliefs have been strengthened, while others have dropped away like autumn leaves.

Walking is the simplest and most human of things. It can be a light, refreshing experience, when we open our shoulders, breathe the air, and enjoy that 'wonderful to be alive' feeling. Or it can create the opportunity to delve deep into our inner lives. For 'thoughtful walking', there is no need to worry about the thinking – thoughts will arise quite naturally. The problem comes with coping with them, and coping too with all those feelings that erupt unbidden – the angers, insecurities and doubts; the distractions, pettinesses and uninvited memories. Walking can stir things up every bit as much as it may calm things down.

An interesting and easy exercise to get the 'thinking and walking' thing going is to ask yourself when walking, 'Is this my body taking my mind for a walk – or is it my mind that is in control and is doing the walking?' Don't fall over!

CHAPTER ONE

THE LONG WALK

A good long walk takes us beyond the horizon — several times. We experience liberation, unique to walking, as countryside or town flow past us at an even, human pace. That hill on the horizon ahead, the church tower or patch of dark woodland — they all grow bigger as we approach them, then drifting past take up a place on the back horizon, finally sinking out of sight. This continual changing of scene is one of the great delights of a long trek.

THE LONG FAMILY WALK

'I absolutely loathe long family walks!' The 10-year-old girl leant forward slightly over my desk to express her fierce opinion. I knew her lovely family well, and her vehemence came as a surprise. I could tell from her expression that she meant every word. But then you get told all sorts of things if you are a school chaplain; not always things that parents would like you to hear!

THE FAMILY WALK — IT IS EASY TO IMAGINE. We have all been through it, I guess: the parents wanting to get a move on; a child at the back dragging its feet. 'Oh, my poor little legs,' as one of my daughters used to mutter, just loud enough to make us feel guilty. Or, at its worst, the very small child who stands stock still, bawling, refusing to budge and demanding to be carried. That often comes after several wheedling attempts have been made, appealing for a lift, arms upheld in hope: 'Up-a Daddy?'

The fact is that walking has to be willingly undertaken. Aching legs, tiredness, soaking rain, even blisters can be borne if one's heart is in it; some mild suffering can even be strangely enjoyable. But children, of whatever age, will feel the pain and resent it, however educational the walk, however uplifting the landscape ('Drink in the view, children!'), if they have not voted for the expedition themselves; 'taken owner-ship', as they say, of its demands.

Despite all that, those of us who enjoy a long walk probably have someone to thank (in my case, probably my mother) for showing us what a wonderful thing walking for pleasure can be, even if we were reluctant converts at first. We can be grateful perhaps for the tactful way they sold us the idea, without dragging us unwillingly out into the wind and the rain. (At the moment of writing, I am feeling particularly proud of my 14-year-old granddaughter, Rose, who, sponsored by her grandmother, is taking part in a 100-mile hike along the Appalachian Way in America. Good for her!)

ON BEING PROPERLY PREPARED
FOR A LONG WALK

It is not enough just to be willing. A good long walk requires some sensible preparation, most of it obvious. Plan the length of the walk with your own past experience in mind. What can you cover comfortably in a day?

MY OWN LIMIT IS ABOUT FIFTEEN TO TWENTY MILES. If you have never done long walks before, then do not be over-ambitious. Be happy with half a dozen miles (or less?) and see how you feel. Build up to a long walk over weeks with several shorter walks, always taking note of your body and how it feels, showing respect for its aches and pains.

CLEAR WATERS RISING

NICHOLAS CRANE
PENGUIN, ISBN 0-14-024332-1

I was impressed by the marathon quality of this challenging long-distance hike – knowing that it is not something I would ever attempt myself, even in my dreams.

Nicholas Crane is now well known to TV viewers in the UK for his appearances, umbrella sticking out of his rucksack, in the series *Coast*. He is an enthusiastic walker par excellence. Just married to the admirable and long-suffering Annabel, Nicholas set off to walk the 10,000 kilometres from Cape Finisterre in Spain to Istanbul, following mountain ranges – the Pyrenees, Alps, Carpathians and the Balkan Mountains. Annabel sends him (or delivers herself) new pairs of boots at regular intervals. My overriding memories of the book are of him trudging wearily through blizzards in search of a place to sleep; and on one occasion totally misreading the contours on a map, so that where he expected a conical mountain he found himself peering down into a deep chasm in pouring rain. It is heartening to find that even the most bold of walkers can make simple mistakes!

I find it valuable to set off with an open heart and mind. It is not a good idea to anticipate solving some major life problem while walking, because that can lead to disappointment and frustration. A relaxed mind is much better, letting thoughts bubble up in their own time.

Preparation Checklist

• First of all, the boots. Footwear is the most important thing to get right; it can make or break a walk. My own boots, worn with thick woollen socks, are so comfortable that it is like putting my feet to bed when I put them on in the morning. After 20 miles they feel the same.

• Tell someone where you are going, if walking by yourself. Get into the habit.

• Pack a light waterproof and a jumper.

• Take food, e.g. banana, energy bar, and some good thick sandwiches.

• Carry a bottle of water. Also a flask of coffee or tea.

• Map (check through your route before setting off).

• Whistle. The sound carries further than a cry for help. You may never need to use it.

• Compass. Make sure you know how to use it! I have only ever needed mine once, when it was invaluable: dark clouds suddenly came down when I was walking over high moorland in Scotland. It is astonishing how disorientating sudden mist and cloud can be.

• A hat (decide for yourself). I wear an old favourite, an Akubra bought years ago in Sydney; it is warm in the cold and rain but protects you from the sun on blazing days. I once lost it in Iceland; miraculously it came back to me.

• Binoculars (optional). I use mine for birds, or sometimes flowers and butterflies on high banks.

• Mobile phone. Half my life's walking was done before these comforting gadgets were invented. Now I always carry one. It was given to me by my son Nat when I returned from a trip to Australia, with the words: 'Dad – I don't want you going off on your own without this!'

GETTING TO KNOW
OUR PLACE IN THE WORLD

The Buddha said, 'You cannot travel on the Path before you have become the Path itself.' He was referring to the Eightfold Path, those aspects of life you have to get right before you can begin to have some understanding of what it means to be human.

THE SAYING HAS APPLICATION TO OUR WALKING, TOO. There is a bond between us and the track; and more than a bond. We and the world we walk through are one. It has become easy for us in the west to forget that fact, particularly if we live our lives surrounded by a host of man-made things, buildings, floors, pavements and streets. We ignore the ground we walk on because it is beneath us.

Our bodies are built from the same soil, grown through the miracle of biochemistry from the minerals that come originally, via plants, from the ground under our feet. Before we were born, all the atoms and molecules that make up our living bodies lay mixed up in the soil. When we die we return to our origins, a process summed up so poignantly in the funeral service: 'Earth to earth, ashes to ashes, dust to dust.' In a mythological sense, the Earth is our mother and father.

We need to foster respect for the path beneath our feet as we walk it. In us, the landscape is observing itself.

Getting to Know My Place

My earliest walking was in the fells of Cumbria (then called 'Cumberland'), where I spent my earliest years. Ancient pink granite outcrops, excitingly veined with white quartz, heave up through the remains of ancestral volcanoes. Mountain crags, half a billion years old, tower over lush green farmland and sheltered homesteads. Lakes radiate out from the central hub of the Scafell Range, where slow-moving blue glaciers gouged out valleys in the past; rocks dropped by retreating ice at the end of the Ice Age still litter the fields today. A massive boulder in my primary school playground in Eskdale had a clog slide down its flank, much used at break time. We would race out of school to the top of the rock and hurtle to the

bottom, sparks flying from clog soles: only later did I come to realize that the slide was a glacial groove carved many millennia before people lived in the valley.

A primary goal in all my walking has been to get to know the world I inhabit. A walking pace is ideal for the purpose and an experience we share with all our ancestors. We are pioneers of evolution, thinking and walking on the surface of the planet. No one has done it ever before in quite the searching and questioning way that we do. Walking in a landscape such as the Lake District, we become aware of the awe-inspiring age of the world, and how recently mankind has scratched an existence from its surface. We are very new.

A CUMBRIAN WALK
FROM SEASCALE TO SCAFELL PIKE

◆

We are new and the world is ancient. A good way to get the feel of this truth is to walk from the coast at Seascale to the highest point in England, Scafell Pike. I know the tracks well and you can do it in a day. Take two if you prefer, and linger as the mood takes you.

THE LANDSCAPE CAN ILLUSTRATE DRAMATICALLY how new the tenancy of modern man is upon the earth. Be prepared for bad weather, even if you set off on this walk in baking sunshine beneath a blue sky. Pack a waterproof in the

knapsack, and a spare jumper. The weather is wonderfully unpredictable in these hills. A hot dry day can turn wet and chilly in the time it takes to eat your sandwiches.

The first thing you may notice, just up the coast, is an industrial installation of buildings and towers protected by a barbed-wire perimeter fence: Sellafield, one of the first nuclear energy plants on the planet. Here, human beings, at the pinnacle of technology, began to harness for the first time the incredible energy locked in the atom, an enterprise not without its dangers. Years ago the plant changed its name from Windscale after an accidental leak of radiation poisoned the countryside around. Is the world safe in our hands? Are we, the new tenants, going to destroy the home planet?

For a couple of miles you walk along a country road flanked by farmland, small hay fields, sheep and cattle, with the magnificent backdrop of the Lakeland fells spread out before you; you are looking up into the jaws of Wasdale, a dark valley on cloudy days, famous for its deep lake and treacherous screes. Scafell Pike is far on the back horizon, with Great Gable and other well-known peaks.

The route takes us through the charming small town of Gosforth – buildings constructed from local red sandstone, colourful gardens with blue hydrangeas, a few small shops – in a matter of minutes; but linger. Already we are walking back into history. A church has stood on the same spot, it is believed, since the 7th century; two rare Viking hogback

tombs rest just beyond the nave as you enter. A tall sandstone Saxon cross, over a thousand years old, stands prominently in the churchyard by the path. The base of the cross is round, tree-like, probably representing Yggdrasil, the World Ash, central to creation in pre-Christian Scandinavian mythology.

Gosforth Cross

The Gosforth Cross is thought to be the tallest ancient cross in Britain, its four sides above the 'trunk' elaborately carved with religious symbols and figures. It takes time to read and interpret these carvings – the entwined snakes, wolf serpents, tiny dynamic warriors and headless monster. What is happening? The tale is a familiar one in the religions of the world, reflecting the universal experience of mankind: the age-old struggle between good and evil.

The particular fascination of the Gosforth Cross is that it can be read as pagan mythology or Christian theology. Is the bound figure the fiend, the trickster god Loki – or the Devil? Is it Odin riding through the hall of serpents and hanging on the tree, self-sacrificed – or Christ crucified, trampling on Satan? The repetition of the Triquetra, the Irish symbol of the Trinity, on all four sides of the column suggests that the craftsmen were primarily inspired by the Christian story, but that they drew on a more ancient symbolism to tell the tale.

The reality of evil is not the first thing that comes to mind when walking in beautiful countryside. But it is something

WANDERLUST: A HISTORY OF WALKING

REBECCA SOLNIT
VIKING, ISBN 0-670-88209-7

It had not occurred to me, before reading this book, that walking might have its own inspiring history. It is so easy to take the activity for granted – rather like breathing. Solnit explores that 'unwritten secret history whose fragments can be found in a thousand unemphatic passages in books, as well as in songs...'. Her research has been thorough and wide-ranging, from poetry to politics. She writes from the heart when recounting the 19th-century rights-of-way battles between working-class people from the polluted industrial cities of northern England, longing for some fresh air in the Derbyshire Peak District, and the gamekeepers of selfish landowners. 'I was thrilled when I got to England and discovered a culture in which trespassing is a mass movement....' The book ends on a sombre note with her own discovery in Las Vegas of the spreading vogue by business to privatize pavements and thoroughfares; security guards replacing gamekeepers in the war against our natural freedom of movement. Where can I sign a petition against this horrible, regressive practice?

we need to consider and take on board if we want to understand our place in the world. Where does it come from and who is to blame?

Is there really a force of evil at loose in the world, 'prowling about seeking whom he may devour' (as described in the late evening service of Compline), which we call the Devil or Satan? There is pain, suffering, disease and death, undoubtedly; and monstrous cruelty too, whether deliberate or the consequence of crass ignorance. But Satan?

It is human nature to look for a figure to blame for our suffering, and for the cruel excesses of mankind; to welcome the existence of a symbol for all that thwarts our good intentions; even to nominate a scapegoat for diverting attention from God when contemplating the tragedies of life. Perhaps Satan is that figure, a magnificent character for the literature of Dante or Milton – but ultimately not real at all, an invention of storytelling, like the Scandinavian trickster Loki.

Cairn Fields

We leave Gosforth by the lane that runs by the River Bleng; it takes us through a bit of forest, up on to the open Stockdale Moor, through bracken and thick tussocks of pale, dry grass. The mountains and crags loom larger ahead.

Here we jump back in time some millennia, long before the Saxons and Vikings inhabited the Gosforth area. A massive oblong pile of stones, nearly thirty metres in length, bears the

name 'Samson's Bratful' on the Ordnance Survey map; a long barrow or burial mound raised to some forgotten chieftain in the Stone Age, five thousand years ago. Legend has it that the stones tumbled here in a heap from the apron of Satan (that old favourite of ancient storytellers!) when he was carelessly casting rocks about the land to make life hard for farmers.

Even more fascinating, to my mind, is the bit of undistinguished moorland a few dozen paces to the south; on the map it is called a cairn field. Here one can really feel in touch with our ancient forebears.

When the first people moved into Cumbria thousands of years ago, after the glaciers had retreated at the end of the last ice age and forests covered the hills, they set about clearing the land using stone axes shaped and polished from local rock. Then they had to clear their small fields of all the stones that had been dragged and dropped from the mountain tops by the ice. They did what gardeners do now – threw the stones into heaps.

Walk slowly back and forth over this bleak bit of moor and there they are, five thousand years later! Some heaps are exposed, while others are low mounds hidden beneath blankets of moss and grass; small cairns in their dozens. Wherever you stand there is a cairn close enough to easily chuck a stone. Stoop and examine them; pick out the odd rock. Someone, ages ago, before the days of Abraham, threw it here into this pile to clear the land for planting grain. I get a greater sense

of kinship with those remote ancestors from standing by their heaps of stones than I ever do at a dramatic site like Stonehenge or Arebury Ring.

Striding across this moor towards Wasdale, I was once startled by a snipe; it rose from my feet with an explosion of wings and flew off in its fast zigzag manner. How clever of evolution, I thought, my heart pounding, to have developed such a marvellous shot-evading strategy in this little game bird. What sport for the guns! Then as I followed its flight admiringly, a peregrine falcon came out of the sun where he had been sailing, waiting for me to flush out a prey, bombed down over the moor in a power dive and narrowly missed his next meal as the snipe ducked into a patch of heather. The evolution of the zigzag flight had nothing to do with hunting guns: peregrines and snipe were developing this arms race long before we appeared on the scene.

Down into the Wasdale Valley

Leaving Stockdale Moor we descend into the valley. As time permits, we visit Nether Wasdale, one of the best-kept villages in the Lake District, and drop into one of its excellent pubs. Then, fortified, we take the track up Cinder Beck past Mill Place, where my brother Inigo lives with his family, and head straight up the centre of Wasdale on an ancient path that weaves between gorse, bracken and bog and seems as old as the rocks that lie about it.

Eventually we reach the lake, Wastwater, for a hard slog on the road for four miles with arguably the most beautiful views in England to each side.

If you have got into your stride, you may now have that familiar sensation when long-distance walking that you are doing nothing, just gazing about, as the landscape flows past you at a gentle three miles an hour, while you remain still. If you have not yet experienced this shift in perspective, then it is worth looking for — a sort of new wakeful awareness. This just has to be the best speed to take in all the passing landscape. Pity the people who stay in their cars.

Where the road skirts the shore we might see a pair of common sandpipers (they are often there), small brown wading birds whose tails bob up and down when they are anxious; they fly off low over the water with a recognizable flight pattern — flick, flick, flick... glide. I only mention them because these solitary little birds seem to turn up wherever I go. I've seen them in Africa, on the coast of Kenya and treading delicately among the crocodiles and hippos in the Masai Mara game reserve; in the Kakadu National Park, Northern Australia; in Queensland and in Perth. Like all other birds, descended as they are from a branch of the dinosaurs, their ancestral history is as noble as is ours. It has taken millions of years for the forces of evolution to shape them so successfully for their place in the environment. We share the world with these beautiful creatures.

At Wasdale Head we cross the stream and head up towards Brown Tongue and the lower flanks of Scafell. Look back at the valley and see that the farmers who moved down from the hills had a harder job to do than the cairn heapers of Stockdale Moor. A thousand years ago the valley bottom would probably have looked like one of the braided rivers of New Zealand. The stream running down from Sty Head Pass would have meandered across the valley bottom, changing its route season by season, leaving banks of gravel and weathered rock. To make their fields the farmers had to do something with all this stone, all these millions of boulders great and small. They developed a skill. The valley became a beautifully controlled chequerboard of green fields separated by the typically Cumbrian dry stone walls, built from gathered stones and held together by no more than gravity and friction. Necessity and toil have produced an art form as great as any installation in a modern gallery.

The Old Coffin Route over the Moor

The track, obviously very old, divides just before you really start climbing. The right fork is the old Coffin Route that runs over a shoulder of Scafell, past Burn Moor Tarn, and then close by a Neolithic stone circle and on down into the village of Boot in Eskdale. For hundreds of years the dead were carried this way for burial in the graveyard at St Catherine's Church by the River Esk. My own father is buried there.

He had the gift of the gab, my Dad, and could tell a funny story – so he would have approved of his funeral. Mercifully we did not have to carry him up over the old Coffin Route – though he would have enjoyed the thought of that. But we were happy to obey his request to be buried in a biodegradable cardboard box, wasting no valuable wood. He asked me to conduct the service, a particularly moving experience since I used to sit in the same priest's pew with him when I was five years old, wrapped in a wing of his cloak, while he conducted evensong for a congregation of six.

What we didn't know was that for some reason his new digital watch had been left on his wrist.

We gathered silently round the grave, hearing the soothing sound of the River Esk as it tumbled over rocks on its way past the churchyard. My brothers stood ready to lower the coffin and I began those clear, telling words that proclaim our kinship with the land we walk upon: 'Earth to earth, ashes to ashes, dust to dust....'

At that moment the alarm on Dad's digital watch went off.

From Nuclear Power Station to Neolithic Axe Factory
The climb we are now taking (following the left fork) becomes steep as a stairway. Many stops for breath are necessary, with a chance to appreciate the view (the one often the excuse for the other!). This is sheep country; open moorland well grazed and good for walking, except where bracken is encroaching.

The introduction of sheep transformed the Lakeland fells a long time ago – they would have been covered in heather and gorse, mountain ash and silver birch. It is one more example of the way humans, in their brief tenancy, by introducing the sheep have changed the surface of the land.

The path levels out beneath the last steep crags of Scafell into a rough tumbled amphitheatre of enormous boulders called Hollow Stones. Earlier in the day we felt we were stepping into the past when walking into the graveyard at Gosforth with its links to the Vikings, and later when wandering through the Neolithic cairn field on Stockdale Moor; but that was nothing. The wild clutter of giant rocks that litter the ground at Hollow Stones were dropped here and left just as they are now at the end of the ice age, when one of the last blocks of glacial ice to cling to a hollow in the hills melted.

It was the work of several ice ages that carved the tops of these mountains into the shapes we now see. The rocks of the crags above us are 450 million years old. We modern humans, Homo sapiens, have been around for much less than a thousandth of that time. The world we arrogantly think we own is so very old and has taken such ages to shape.

The site of a Stone Age axe factory nestles at the foot of these crags, somewhere beneath Pulpit Rock. High quality volcanic stone axes were being cut and polished here, and then exported as far as the continent long before the Christian era. Swing your head round and check our progress since those

early days before writing was invented or the great religions of the world created. There, down on the coast, is the nuclear power station at Sellafield.

From Neolithic axe factory to nuclear power station in one glance. For all our human history of cairn fields and wall building, sheep grazing and ploughing we have just scratched the surface of the planet. We are so very new.

At the summit you feel you are at the top of the world. You may see the lowlands of Scotland at Annan and the mountains of North Wales. The Isle of Man, a blue silhouette, sails on the distant horizon of the Irish Sea; Cumbrian peaks stand all around. Half hidden by moorland, and way below, are the valleys where my sister and brothers and I spent much of our childhood, Eskdale and Seathwaite in Dunnerdale. The rim of the valley was the horizon of our small world. As a child I could not imagine that anything lay beyond the dark flanks of Black Combe at the foot of Dunnerdale.

If the day is hot, you might like to reward yourself by stripping off and swimming in a pool of the beck that runs back down into Wasdale. Fresh bubbling water, crystal clear tumbles in white torrents from pool to pool, surrounded by ferns and mountain ash. The views are magnificent. I shared this unbeatable experience once with my 15-year-old daughter Natasha, who, with her younger brother Josh, had just climbed Scafell in record time. The very same daughter who, when much younger, complained of her poor little legs!

A WALK FROM LONDON
TO THE SOURCE OF THE RIVER THAMES

That Cumbrian walk covers old ground for me. I know every bit of it well. But the habitual walker is never content with sticking to familiar ground and I often want to stray on to new tracks and explore new territory.

AFTER LIVING IN LONDON FOR MANY YEARS, I decided to explore the River Thames and walk from the tidal barrier at Woolwich to the source in a field near Kemble, only three miles or so from where I lived as a curate in Cirencester. The end and the beginning were already familiar, but I knew very little of the river's meandering journey through Middlesex, Berkshire, Oxfordshire and Gloucestershire.

There is something deeply satisfying about walking the course of a river, discovering its character, observing its changes as it flows down to the mouth. There are many ways to get to know the Thames by boat or towpath. Some people like to do it all in a week, planning their B&Bs in advance, either heading down to the sea from the Cotswolds, or starting at the Thames Estuary and walking inland. I hear only good reports of that method.

My own way was to walk the Thames in stages, mostly on my own, over a period of about a year. My son Nat took a day off work to join me for one stretch of towpath in Oxford-

shire, through fields of hay and corn and along lanes lined with poplars. We were keen to see Kelmscott Manor where William Morris lived, father of the Arts and Crafts Move ment. He also lived in a house by Hammersmith Bridge, Kelmscott House, only minutes from our own home. In his *News from Nowhere* he fantasizes about a pure socialist utopia where money is abolished and young people give their labour for free, rowing up the Thames in late summer to gather in the harvest.

The Changing World

It was one of the poplars by the Thames not far from Kelm-scott Manor that opened my mind to how our world has changed since I was a boy.

'That poplar there!' I said. 'It's not a Lombardy poplar like the others, it's a … Oh dear, I can't remember the name.' I stood for some moments racking my brains for a word I knew I knew. 'The leaves have flat stalks so that they tremble and quake in the breeze. There! Look now how they shiver!"

Nat was fiddling with his iPhone, checking a message I guessed, taking no interest in my observations.

'How about "aspen" – is that the word you were looking for?' he asked, seconds later, waving his mobile.

I was dumbfounded. 'How did you find that?'

'I just got onto the internet and typed in "poplar" – look, here's the list of all the different types, with their Latin names.

The things I was discovering on the riverbank!

My method for Thames walking was simple and required minimal planning. I would wait for good weather and decide the night before to cover another dozen or so miles the next day. Using train or bus, sometimes both, I could easily rejoin the towpath where I had left off the previous time. Only twice did I need to use my car – and a couple of times a taxi back to a bus stop (this was when a mobile phone came in handy). By always choosing good days, my memory of the Thames is flooded in glorious sunshine!

ON ALERTING ALL THE SENSES

An undertaker in Yorkshire always gave me notice of when he would be away on vacation. Each year he would take a walking holiday with a blind cousin and they would tackle the River Thames, the Downs or the Pennine Way together.

YOU KNOW, VICAR, IT'S AMAZING,' he said to me once, 'my cousin gets as much out of walking as I do, even though he's blind – often as not he'll tell me about the birds we pass before I even see them!'

Walking mindfully involves more than just watching the country flow by. All our senses should be involved. A blind man is alert to the call of birds – and we can be, too. There are

the sounds of the wind, differing from tree to tree; of running water, infinitely variable; distant dogs barking; birds singing. And there is the feeling of wind, sun and rain on the skin as we walk through changing weather. And let us not ignore all the ever-changing smells – the sweet scent of honeysuckle or the warmly coconut smell of gorse in full bloom; the richly pungent smells wafting from the farmyard; the aroma of loam, rotting leaves, and wet earth. Can you beat the smell of newly mown hay drifting from a field newly harvested? All these sensual experiences must be allowed full play.

You may have noted that my notes 'On being properly prepared for a long walk', at the beginning of the chapter, did not include an iPod or headphones. I find it difficult to understand why one would want such a distraction when walking. When walking – walk! But I suppose that is a personal matter.

I am not *totally* opposed to listening to music while walking. Many years ago I climbed Scafell with a group of young offenders from the city. They were so very far out of their comfort zone that we allowed them to carry a transistor radio (that's how long ago it was!); and they dribbled a football from Wasdale Head to the top of Scafell Pike, something that no one had done before!

REJECTING THE SLAVE MASTER, HASTE

I moved from London a few years ago to live with my partner Ros in the medieval village of Alfriston in East Sussex. Our home lies within a hundred yards of the South Downs Way, the old pilgrim route from Eastbourne to the cathedral at Winchester, burial place of pre-Norman kings.

HAVING COMPLETED THE LENGTH OF THE THAMES from my home in Hammersmith, I now have another long but local trail to explore. Already, as I write, I am half done; but I am using a different method from that used for the Thames. Once again I am walking the way in stages, not attempting it in one go or using B&Bs. The first couple of sections involved no organization at all. A bus to Eastbourne presented me with a comfortable day's walk back home, via the coast and the rolling track along the tops of the white chalk cliffs known as the Seven Sisters. A month later I walked on west from my front door, over Firle Beacon and down into Lewes after crossing the River Ouse. A lift got me home.

From there on I resorted to using the car. This presented a problem – how to get back to the car after a day's hike. Buses are few and far between; taxis would be expensive. A prejudice had to be overcome that each section should be a good day's walk to the west towards Winchester, always picking up the track where I had left it and moving on.

The answer was simple. Park the car, walk half a dozen miles, have a picnic and then walk back to the car. This way I do the South Downs Way twice, once in each direction! It will take longer – but what does that matter? What a relief!

I am glad I overcame the 'getting on with it' prejudice and the unnecessary sense of haste. Walking back over the same track covered in the morning has a distinct benefit; you see the view in reverse under different lighting, and absorb it again, noticing much more than before. I often wonder about my undertaker's cousin and what he would 'see' of the South Downs in his blindness. The experience, I am sure, was as fulfilling for him as for me, only different.

Unlike following the course of a river, walking the Downs involves a lot of up and down work as the path, rising to the gently curving tops, presents you with tremendous views and wide horizons. From the ancient hill fort of Chanctonbury Ring you see a splendid sweep of the English Channel from Beachy Head to the Isle of Wight. Skylarks sing everywhere, proclaiming their territory with wild beauty (at one spot only five miles from the centre of Brighton). We can be grateful that there are now pressure groups, such as the RSPB, who work energetically for the preservation of the habitat of these wonderful birds; otherwise, we will lose them for ever. The preservation of habitats of species other than our own has become one of the pressing moral imperatives of our age, an obligation we are only just beginning to face in the 21st

century. To think that a creature that has taken millions of years to evolve should be lost to the world because of our carelessness is truly terrible.

From these uplands the path regularly plunges down again through steep woods and old deep holloways, or sunken lanes, to cross the Rivers Cuckmere, Ouse, Adur or Arun. In some of these valleys, among the hayfields and corn, the cattle and old cottages, and the flint-built churches, their spires poking above sheltering trees, you can imagine you are exploring a painting by one of my favourite English artists, Samuel Palmer.

TRANSFIGURATION

◆

The tiny church at Pyecombe in the valley of the A23 is worth a visit if only for its unusual dedication – 'The Downland Church of the Transfiguration'. The name of the church refers, of course, to a central event in the Gospel stories.

PETER, JAMES AND JOHN climb a mountain with Jesus; there they are astonished by a vision in which Jesus is transfigured, his garments shining brilliantly white, 'whiter than any earthly bleacher could make them'. They saw something in him they had missed until then, thinking of him only as a rabbi or prophet. Now they were overcome with the conviction that he was more than that. His relationship with the

Divine was intimate. In him they came close, they believed, to the glory of God; they felt a deeper significance in their lives that they had not felt before.

The Gospel tale is very formal in its telling. Moses and Elijah appear in the vision, representing the Law and the Prophets (traditional Jewish religion), and a voice speaks from heaven. We shall never know how much the story has been worked over in the telling, whether it is an elaboration of a recollection, or an accurate memory of a vision.

A Transcendent 'Beyond'

However we read it, the story of the Transfiguration is powerfully symbolic. It speaks to us of a transcendent 'Beyond' always waiting to break through into our consciousness. Rather like the feeling you might get listening to Monteverdi in a Norman cathedral. And I find it interesting to remember that the disciples were on a walk with Jesus, away from the crowds, when they had their transfiguration experience.

I think that this potential for waking up to deeper spiritual truths and realities is there throughout life. Mostly it gets suppressed by day-to-day routines, by familiarity and by laziness. We take life for granted much too easily. We need to 'break out' a bit; and going for a walk can be a very good way to do that. Walking mindfully a new path in the country, one can sometimes experience transfiguration, discover a deeper layer of life beneath the everyday.

CHAPTER TWO

WALKING IN AUSTRALIA

*There is something about walking in the
Australian bush that makes me return again and
again. The sense of space, the big open skies, the clarity
of the air are unique in my experience; and the vibrant
colours of the birds vie with the rainbow. The red
earth is always richer than I remember and the
sky bluer, hitting the horizon in a hard line.
The land is marvellously ancient, making even
my own Cumbria appear young.*

The Human Race

A TV programme caught my attention during my first visit to Australia: *The Human Race*. An inspired producer, early in the days of reality TV, had hit on a brilliant piece of entertainment – a walking race, five hundred miles across the uninhabited Kimberley Desert in the north of Western Australia. The three competitors started their journey from an ancient meteor crater with no more than they could personally take with them. One was a German survival expert, pulling a trolley with his water tank; the second a young American marathon runner, fit and quite used to the desert heat. The third was an Aboriginal grandfather, apparently carrying nothing. The walkers were monitored every few days by a non-interfering camera team who came and went by helicopter.

I hardly need to tell you who won: the Aboriginal grandfather. He had grown up with a people who taught him to feel at one with the land. The Australian bush was not an alien place for him; the wilderness was home and he belonged to its soil. The practice of mindful walking came to him naturally. He knew where to find water by watching the birds flocking in the evening and he could find food by digging for roots. He was more attune to the surrounding world through his practice of mindfulness.

My First Steps Out into the Bush

---◆---

I was in Sydney, doing the odd bit of teaching in Ascham School, Edgecliff, and longing to get out into the bush, excited at the prospect and promise of seeing new birds. My preconceived images of Australia came from the paintings of Sidney Nolan (the escapades of Ned Kelly) and the novels of Patrick White. I thought that I knew what to expect.

NOTHING COULD HAVE PREPARED ME for what I discovered. It was a revelation. My first immersion in the bush came with an 18-mile hike through the Royal National Park south of Botany Bay. I caught an early morning train from Sydney to Waterfall with the plan to walk back through the wilderness of forest and bush, the rocks and wild scrub around the Hacking River, to the station at Loftus. To taste the wilderness, you really do need to walk on your own. I carried plenty of water, a good route map and a whistle. I left a note at the school to say where I was going.

The bizarre fluting of Australian magpies (they sound like angels gargling) accompanied me as I walked down the road to the start of the wilderness track. From the familiar – the shops, the morning coffee, Australian accents on the train, the ordinary metalled road – I was hiking into strange new territory. After an hour's walking through the forest I stopped. An apricot-breasted, soft grey cuckoo, which I had never seen

before, flew in to perch on a low limb just ahead of me. At that moment a white-bellied eagle circled high beyond a gap in the trees.

I turned and looked all around me with a growing feeling of astonishment and a welling emotion of gratitude and well-being. Everything was unfamiliar. I could have been dropped onto an alien planet. I studied the trees. Not one could I name — no beech, elm or oak, no familiar ash or birch. Everything was very strange.

It was one of the most fulfilling moments of my life, making me toy with the thought that that is why we are here; to look around the world in our short lives of wakefulness, see how it is getting on, and delight in its presence and rich biodiversity.

Mindful Observation

I never carry a bird book with me, preferring to think long and hard about what I have seen and then consult my book at the end of the day. The return to the bird book with a cargo of memories is itself one of the great thrills of walking for me.

The apricot-breasted bird turned out to be a fantailed cuckoo; and the eagle, a white-bellied sea eagle. But the trees took me longer to learn. There were banksias with orange bottlebrush flowers and rough bark, like badly burnt apple crumble (a forest fire in 1994 had left many trunks of charred charcoal); the scribble gums looked as though a child had gone wild with a pencil all over their trunks — the tracks of

insects revealed when the gum tree annually sheds its bark. Among the strangest were the pink-barked angophoras, their smooth twisted limbs sticking out at odd angles like elbows.

Oddest were the slow-growing grass trees, popularly known as Black Boys (now a politically unacceptable term). Blackened by the regular forest fires, these gnarled stumps, as tall as a man, only add a foot in height in a hundred years. After fire they sprout a fresh green wig of grass and a spear for a flower. A grass tree only four feet high pre-dates in age the arrival of Captain Cook on these shores and the naming of Botany Bay. Again I had that familiar feeling I get when confronted by nature – it was all here before we were.

AUSTRALIAN ARTISTS

A visit to the Art Gallery of New South Wales in Sydney opened my eyes to artists other than Sidney Nolan and helped me learn how to look at the Australian landscape when walking. Images of small homesteads and enormous eucalyptus trees, red earth, white tussocks of spinifex and untidy scrub, sheep shearers and distant blue horizons covered the walls.

I WAS BEGINNING TO GRASP THE EXTRAORDINARY SPACE that is Australia, and the unique light. A painting of the 1890 flooding of the Darling River kept pulling me back to look again; it draws the eye, past some sacred ibis in the foreground, and miles into a vast flooded plain dotted with trees, to a far horizon untidy with clouds.

Untidiness; the *beauty* of untidiness was beginning to take hold of me. Many of the first European settlers hated the chaotic scrub of the wild bush, the drought-tolerant Mulga and the twisted shrub-like mallee gum, the wattles and fire-blackened eucalypts; the untidy paper-barks. Around Melbourne they tried to recreate an English landscape, with organized farmland, fields and European trees. But the bush has its own addictive beauty.

Arthur Boyd captures wonderfully the character of the Australian bush in his painting *The Expulsion* – Adam and Eve are driven through a wild thicket of untidy thorn bush by an angry angel, while a crow-like currawong mocks them. It has to be one of the most powerful pictures I know.

A temporary exhibition of Aboriginal art introduced me to the earth colours of Australia – rich red and terracotta, ochre, cream and deep brown.

William Robinson's *Creation*

One artist perplexed and fascinated me. William Robinson, a Brisbane man, explores in his paintings the eucalyptus forests of the Blue Mountains and the rainforests of Queensland. One vast canvas, a triptych, is called *Creation*. It is a wonderful turmoil of trees and ferns. Twisting trunks lie or stretch this

way and that; the sky appears below the forest floor, while unexpected horizons fall at odd angles; there are spider's webs and stars reflected in forest pools. It was only later when I walked in the Blue Mountains that I understood what was happening in Robinson's work. I returned to the gallery weeks later, looked again and marvelled.

THE BLUE MOUNTAINS

The rail map showing the stations between Sydney and the Blue Mountains contains an entertaining jumble of names given nostalgically by settlers from England: Penrith and Blackheath, Bathurst and Woodford. I took the train to Katoomba and explored from there.

THE RAIL LINE FOLLOWS THE RIDGES of the mountain, which gives the European hiker the odd experience, when mountain climbing, of starting at the top and walking down into the valleys then back up to the top at the end of the day (confirming the childhood prejudice that everything in Australia is upside down!)

I was hoping to see a lyrebird, the emblem of Australia; they are tremendous mimics and imitate at will the kookaburra's laugh, the whip-crack explosive sound of the eastern whipbird, the squawk of parrots, the calls of honeyeaters – even the sound of cameras rewinding film and of chainsaws.

Local lyrebirds made a speciality of mimicking the 'ping' of a hammer driving a nail into rock where a metal staircase, over a generation before, had been bolted to the cliff.

On Being Overwhelmed

This is not a place to walk far on your own, even with a whistle, the risk of getting lost being great. So having descended a steep staircase, I ventured only a short way out into the forest along a clearly marked track. A waterfall cascaded so far down the cliffs behind me that it turned into spray, drenching the rocks below with continuous rain; ferns flourished. The forest wrapped itself around me, enveloping me in undergrowth, towering trunks and the blue haze of eucalyptus leaves. New birds revealed themselves: firetails and fantails, eastern yellow robins and crimson rosella parakeets. A scarlet Australian king parrot with bright green wings landed above me. It was hard to take it all in.

William Robinson's painting *Creation* came to mind; and I understood. When you walk in this forest you feel so overwhelmed that your head turns in every direction all the time; looking up the majestic trunks of trees or down to their buttressed roots; following the flight of a colourful parakeet through the canopy; peering into the bush at bush wrens (close associates of lyrebirds – they scratch the forest floor together); turning over your shoulder at the crack of a twig; catching a view of the cliffs above: rocks, trees, sky, ground;

up, down, behind, before. All this turning and twisting of the head builds up a complete, mixed panoramic view, of a rich organic world. Robinson's cleverness was to include all these various perspectives in one great painting. He had painted the holistic *experience of walking* in the forest and not just the scene. I couldn't wait to get back to look at it again.

Meanwhile I had just discovered that getting lost is not the only hazard to be faced on a forest walk. Preoccupied with a wealth of new birds to identify, I had neglected to watch where I was putting my feet and only just happened to look down in time. A red-bellied black snake lay coiled in the path eyeing me. He blocked my way. We stared at each other for what seemed like minutes. Then the snake did the decent thing and slid off to the side of the path and disappeared beneath a log. I vowed to treat all logs with caution after that.

An Unexpected Encounter

In the evening, having climbed back up to the top of the Blue Mountain ridge, I loitered for some moments to watch the sunset sky down a long firebreak in the forest. I was tired, happy, but I hadn't seen a lyrebird.

Suddenly there was movement among the ferns and a pheasant-sized bird, the colour of blue shadows and the brown loam of the forest floor, strolled out into the open. He trailed a delicately feathery tail.

'Oh! Thank you!' I whispered.

WALKING WITH GRATITUDE

◆

I had come by now to recognize this welling sense of gratitude as I walked through the forest and bush — but gratitude to whom? The immediate answer, I suppose, is God.

SAYING PRAYERS IS A NATURAL ACTIVITY FOR ME. But what can we say about God? The Mystery that lies in and beyond these ancient Australian landscapes, and wherever else I walk, the Source of all evolving life, is the God I approach tentatively when I whisper, 'Lord – thank you!'

Far away from Europe I had gained a new perspective on God, creator, the focus of my gratitude, the Source of all this. In the Judeo-Christian-Muslim west we have tied God down to a small piece of recent history, limited him to the narrative of our own tribal story, and packaged him within the close horizons of western culture.

A New Perspective

Walking here in the bush had helped me liberate my ideas about God. I like the language that speaks of God as the Ground of all Being. God is the Source of 'all *this*', of everything I know about, and everything I shall never know about; the Power, the Life, the Mind, creating this whole, ancient, vast and evolving universe. He (for want of a better personal pronoun) is the Ultimate Reality that lies behind all that we

see. Without him the Blue Mountains would not be; nor the blue fairy wren, the lyrebird, nor me.

I am increasingly convinced that the Christian churches have become careless in the way they have led people to think of God. A misreading of those wonderful creation stories in Genesis (parables, not scientific accounts) has led us to think of God creating once in the distant past, 'in the beginning'. But if He *is* the Source of all things, then He is creating now – every moment of today. The definition of God written by the French mystic Simone Weil appeals to me: 'God is he in whose wake the year unfolds its days.' God walks ahead of me.

Fundamentalists in many evangelical churches read the Genesis creation stories as though they were literally true; God creating everything in six days about six thousand years ago. This will be seen eventually as an aberration in Christian history, I believe, and not the way this piece of scripture was intended to be read. Ironically, by idolizing the wise scribbling of our forebears, they treat scripture in a way that is a form of idolatry, thus breaking the second commandment. Fundamentalists miss out on a whole wealth of wisdom that accrues to acknowledging our part in an evolving world.

OUR RESPONSIBILITIES FOR THE
NATURAL WORLD & ITS BIODIVERSITY

◆

What are we to do when we come to recognize this spiritual reality? When we come to acknowledge that a creative spiritual power is responsible for the biodiversity of the evolving world around us? It makes demands of us. We cannot ignore the fact that as humans we have moral responsibilities.

A PROPHET WHOSE WORDS ARE RECORDED in the Old Testament gives a good answer. Micah lived nearly three thousand years ago in Judea; he was appalled by the uncaring ways of his contemporary society and their false ideas about religion. The answer he gives to the question of how to live the good life is simple: '*Seek Justice; practise kindness and walk humbly with God.*' That is all. It is enough.

We can apply Micah's definition to the natural world we inhabit. The world is not ours to exploit for our own purposes. Coupled with deep wisdom and insight in the Genesis creation stories, there is also some arrogance in the early chapters of the Bible that has misled us into believing that we have dominion over nature. Perhaps such arrogance was necessary, when as a species we first began to wake up to our powers (I shall have to think about that); but not now. We have the privilege of consciousness, an appreciation of beauty, and have developed immense technical abilities; perhaps we are

even the pioneers of the evolutionary process: that, however, gives us no right to behave with the dominating will of an uncaring landlord.

Dreaming of Creation

The Aboriginal people of Australia had their own gentle relationship with the soil and with the rest of Nature, before we Europeans arrived. They had their own lovely, and original idea that the world was created through walking.

They believed it had been sung into existence in the Dreamtime by their totemic ancestors, who walked about creating the landscape through song as they went; this rocky outcrop, that billabong, the gum tree, mallee bush and tufts of spinifex. These ancient invisible routes criss-cross Australia and are rehearsed again and again by each generation who memorize and pass on chunks of the ancestral song. Their relationship with the land was personal and intimate; they knew that they were part of the land and identified with it.

A sense of gratitude comes naturally, I find, as I walk in the Australian bush. It bubbles up unbidden. I now understand Micah better. When we walk, we should walk humbly. Humbly not just in the presence of God but humbly in the presence of other living things.

WALKING NEAR SACRED SITES

◆

The sense of the sacred tends to be limited in Europe to the sanctu-
aries of churches and cathedrals — and for some people to pre-Chris-
tian sites like Stonehenge. Not so in many other parts of the world.

I N THE USA, NATIVE AMERICANS have their sacred mountains; the Japanese erect torii arches in the countryside to
proclaim a lake, grove or hill sacred; while in Australia the
Aboriginals have many sacred sites throughout the land associated with their Songlines.

In the developed world we have lost an awareness of this
sort of relationship with the land. We ignore the world we
walk on because it is beneath us.

I flew from Sydney to one of the great sacred sites in the
Red Centre, Uluru; flying first to Alice Springs and then
taking a coach ride out to the rock on another day. In Alice I
had the minor personal satisfaction of identifying a bird that
landed on a ghost gum by the dried-up riverbed of the Todd.
It flew and looked like a cuckoo, perched like a shrike and had
a black face. On returning to my bird book that evening it
turned out to be a black-faced cuckoo shrike!

The Sacred Site of Uluru

I stayed at the resort at Uluru, and got a lift out to the Rock
for a day's walk anticlockwise around its base. There is a

footpath and the walker can enjoy almost perfect solitude for the six miles (or you could in 1997 when I did it). Most visitors prefer to hang around the cultural centre or the car park, a few attempting the rather precarious looking climb to the top (a practice frowned upon by the Anangu, for whom it is sacred). I was content to stay at ground level.

THE SONGLINES

BRUCE CHATWIN
VINTAGE CLASSICS, ISBN 978-0-099-76991-0

It was this book that made me determined to go walking in the Australian bush and to see for myself something of its famous Red Centre. I was intrigued by the extraordinary relationship, explored by the author, between the Australian Aboriginal and the land they have inhabited for so many thousands of years back to the Dreamtime. Chatwin believes that Natural Selection has designed us humans – from the structure of our brain cells to the structure of our big toe – for a career of seasonal journeys on foot through a blistering landscape of thorn-scrub or desert. This conjecture brings him to Alice Springs at the heart of the continent to talk with some fascinating characters about the Songlines of the local Aboriginals. These Songlines are the invisible pathways that criss-cross Australia, pathways that the ancestors walked in the beginning when they created the land by singing it into existence. The singer, the song and the track become one.

Named Ayers Rock by Europeans, this massive natural monument has been given back its original name 'Uluru' and is one of the great success stories of the Aboriginal communities. Treated for so long with utter distain, they have now acquired a voice to speak for their rights and there is a growing respect for their culture.

Traditionally, Uluru is a site of sacred initiation rituals through which boys become men; a pool at the foot of the cliffs is associated with the Earth Mother and is sacred to women. Every cleft, ravine and cave is celebrated in song and chant that date back to the Dreamtime; every boulder has a legend attached to it; Serpent myths abound. Despite its importance, the Aboriginals welcome visitors – provided, of course, they show respect and understanding.

THE AGE OF AUSTRALIA

◆

The visitor to Australia does not have to be around for long to realize how old the continent is. It broke away from the supercontinent Gondwanaland half a billion years ago into its current isolation.

SOME OF THE CRATON BASEMENT ROCK is so ancient it is nearly as old as the planet itself, floating for more than three and a half billion years on the Earth's mantle. Even the Aboriginals, who have been around for fifty thousand years, are

newcomers to the land. We are all like ants, briefly scurrying on its old crumbling surface, its ancient weathered landscape.

Dry white spinifex grows in tufts on the orange desert, reminiscent of an aboriginal painting, and the blue sky hits the Rock in a hard clear line. The colours of the rock are as extravagant as anything printed in a tourist brochure; a thousand feet of weathered sandstone, shaped into curves and gullies through the ages by the weather – wind, rain and sandstorm. Iron gives the baked crumbling crust its rich reds and oranges, which turn purple in the evening light.

Turn away from the Rock and the bush spreads out to the wide horizon like an ocean   wattle, thorn bush and spear-like desert oak; tiny bright flowers, such as the desert pea, hug the ground. I would love to have walked out into that wilderness where nothing changes for a thousand miles. Robyn Davidson did this on her own, trekking from Alice to the Indian Ocean north of Perth. She gives an account of the journey in her book *Tracks*. A bit of me is very envious.

The Here and Now
By standing still I was fortunate to see a red-capped robin, some black-faced wood swallows, a bellbird and several hawks. I was stunned to watch flocks of budgerigars fly overhead like shoals of green fish in a deep blue sea. Sometimes as many as a hundred would flash through the bush together, chattering excitedly, converging on a waterhole. It was their

TRACKS

ROBYN DAVIDSON

PICADOR, ISBN 0-330-36861-3

I met Robyn Davidson at a London supper party and quickly became an astonished admirer, ordering a copy of *Tracks* from my local bookshop the very next day. In an epic journey, recounted in the book, Robyn walks and rides nearly two thousand miles through deserts and bush, from Australia's Red Centre to the Indian Ocean; with her are three camels and a dog. Elation alternates with loneliness; 'All I remember of that first day alone was a feeling of release; a sustained, buoyant confidence as I strolled along...', while later, when temporarily lost, she writes, 'I felt very small and very alone suddenly, in this great emptiness. I could climb a hill and look to where the horizon shimmered blue into the sky and see nothing. Absolutely nothing.' Davidson needed the ordeal to sort out some aspects of her life and found that 'strange things do happen when you trudge twenty miles a day, day after day, month after month'. She was able to explore relationships from her past, way back to childhood, and discovered in the process a new, detached happiness. A great tribute to walking!

world, not mine, a world of freedom without people, far from that isolated cage in a pet shop.

Innumerable honeyeaters whistled out in the bush, gathering nectar. It was watching one of these, the humble singing

honeyeater, that I experienced again that overwhelming sense of contentment and well-being; that feeling of 'I want to be nowhere else. Just here, in this moment, *this* is what I am for — *here* and *now*.'

To stand there and feel absorbed into the scene was enough; to see the bird on its bottlebrush flower, the Rock, the sky; and to feel gratitude. It felt like a transfiguration where the inner world of the soul and the outer realm of rock and burgeoning life came together in oneness. I could have been tempted to use the language of vision, and say simply 'I see!'

ALL CREATURES, EVEN THOSE THAT BITE!

They cloud around your head, a stationary halo when you rest; they become fellow travellers as you walk. The 'Australian wave' is an automatic and fruitless response. Then there are tormenting mosquitoes in the tropical parts of the continent. They can be hard to bear.

WALKING IN FARAWAY PLACES is not always comfortable and I do not want to end this chapter with the idea that mindful walking is punctuated by exclusively beautiful moments! While I encountered plenty of flies and mosquitoes in Australia, my most challenging experience of them was on another continent when I stayed with friends on their cattle ranch in Paraguay. A half-swampy landscape of palm savannah offered great opportunities to see new birds. I was particularly eager to find the scissor-tailed tyrant, a romantically named soft grey flycatcher that sports a divided tail longer than its own body; it appeared in a King Penguin *Birds of La Plata* that I had won as a form prize at school when I was 12 years old, more than fifty years ago.

The bird-life was as rich as I had anticipated; and the mosquito-life was militant. They hovered in clouds and could drill through any clothing. In the humid heat I wore borrowed wellington boots, a jacket tied tight at the sleeves and a hat pulled well down. Passing gauchos, straight-legged in their saddles, smiled as they rode effortlessly by — or was it a smirk?

There were woodpeckers galore (three species in one thorn bush); roseate spoonbills; herons in all shapes, sizes and colours; and caiman alligators in the ditches. And mosquitoes were just everywhere.

I saw vermillion flycatchers, their plumage startlingly red in the green bush, and pure white flycatchers called white monjitas, which looked and fluttered like elegant moths. Finally, a scissor-tailed tyrant flopped in undulating flight over some grassland and perched on a fence. Its scissor tail opened and closed as it landed.

I had waited half a century for this moment.

It became a powerful exercise in restraint, to hold my binoculars still as several grateful mosquitoes set about feeding on my hands, about my eyebrows and in my ears!

In Praise of the Insect

South America has more than 130 species of flycatcher (we have only two in England). Their colourful diversity is stunning. But for all that richness we have to pay a price, and to thank part of their diet – the mosquito.

On the whole, we tend to think of insects as one of the great irritations of life – whether wasps, midges, bluebottles or mosquitoes. We are happy about butterflies because they are beautiful (but even they lay their eggs on our vegetables, giving rise to our summer warfare against hungry caterpillars). And we don't mind bees because they give us honey. But the biting, nibbling, stinging that goes with all the rest we could gladly do without.

Insects are the most successful class of animals on earth; there are more species of insect than of any other creature. It can truly be said that this is their world. They have a supremely important role to play in the planet's ecosystem; without them, most of our fruit trees would not be pollinated, and an awful lot of insect-eating birds would become extinct. An insect-free world would be a disaster. I remind myself of this whenever a mosquito decides to drill into my hand as I struggle to hold my binoculars still.

'RESPECT FOR INSECTS' and 'HANDS OFF MOSQUITOES' are not placards I am ever likely to see at a public demonstration, unfortunately. One can but dream.

CHAPTER THREE

CITY WALKING

The pavements can be hard and tiring, but walking in a city has more to offer than we often imagine. The city is not all streets and pavements; there are parks and public gardens, river walks and canal banks. The richness and variety of experiences per mile in a city can challenge even the most beautiful walk through countryside; and the density of wild bird-life, flowers and trees is a continual surprise.

POUNDING THE CITY STREETS

For many people, the thought never seems to occur that the city is a great place for walking. They imagine that you have to get out of the city, away from the noise, the traffic and the fumes and head for the countryside where birds sing and brooks sparkle. They could not be more wrong.

O F COURSE, IT IS GREAT TO GET OUT into the open country, but I do know people who have made the exodus, lock, stock and barrel, and found themselves living by fields with barbed-wire fences, bad-tempered farmers with locked gates and inaccessible lanes, muddy tracks waiting to drag the unwary into glutinous depths, and only a main road to walk on, dominated by speeding commuters all hell-bent on driving a walker up the bank. Come back to the peace, calm and birdsong of the city – and all its other attractions! You only have to know where to look.

Any good bookshop in a city will have a travel section and a selection of books on walking in the area. You can explore whatever takes your fancy, from a tour of architecture to a crawl round the best pubs; from recent history to ancient archaeology. The ghosts of the city are waiting for you at every corner. Only on foot can you meet them properly.

I have one such guide in my hand now: *Walking the London Scene; Five Walks in the Footsteps of the Beat Generation*, by Sydney

---

Famous City Walkers

When you walk through a city, with the purpose of just walking, you join a venerable group of people who have done the same, each with their own particular needs. Soren Kierkegaard, the existentialist Christian thinker, who influenced many theologians of my generation, pounded the streets of Copenhagen because he could only think when surrounded by the noise and distractions of the city. Charles Dickens, even more famously, would walk at night, sometimes tramping through to dawn. He craved violent exercise 'to still his beating mind' and calm his restless energy. The writing of *Bleak House* made him so anxious he had to take regular 20-mile walks through the city in order to quieten or exhaust his restless spirit.

R Davies. Here you can follow Kerouac, in thought, into the old, now demolished, King Lud pub at Ludgate Circus 'for a sixpenny Welsh rarebit and a stout' (it would cost him a bit more now!).

Look Up!

If I had to give one piece of advice on city walking, it would be: 'Look up!' It is easy to be distracted on the street by the hustle and bustle of pedestrians, the hassle of the traffic, the

need to get from here to there; the shop windows and the captivating smells; the coffee shops, the soap shops, the passing perfumes and cigars. We get caught up in a two-metre layer of fascinating, noisy, human activity.

Look at the rooftops and gables, the detailed ornamentation around the windows; the carved brickwork and statues; the tiling and chimney design; the clocks and stained glass high above street level. Someone has designed and created every feature, with care and skill. They deserve to have their work admired from the pavement. No one needs to be an architect to appreciate it all.

Every city has its own unique character and, by looking up, you begin to acquire a taste for the differences. No city I know demands more that the pedestrian look up than New York. I doubt if anyone can walk down Fifth Avenue without raising the eyes and gasping at the astonishing world soaring hundreds of feet above street level. The buildings draw the eye up above the taxis and flashing lights at pedestrian crossings. Art deco challenges mock gothic across the street; ornamental brick vies with glass; pinnacles, towers and gargoyles seem to dream of another era and of another place, a high-up world where the sun sets later than it does down on the pavement.

THE RADIAL WALK: STARTING FROM HOME

The great thing about the radial city walk is that it always starts at your own front door. The city is spread out around you; your home, as far as you are concerned, is at the heart of it.

WHATEVER YOUR AREA — centre, suburb, west end or city block — your home is the pivot, the axis; the place you look out from; from here you view the city both in your mind and through your windows. From your point of view, your perspective, the city extends in every direction away from your home. This is where your mind always comes home to roost.

So, you shut your door and, given the state of things today, probably lock it, and set off walking in any direction. You may have packed some sandwiches, an apple and a flask of coffee; or you may have decided to travel light and hope to find a cafe or a pub at the right time. Finding food and drink is not a problem in a city. It would be advisable to consult a tube, bus or train map and timetable before setting off on your urban adventure. One of the bonuses of city walking is the ease with which you can get home in time for tea or a shower and your own bed; it depends only on a little planning.

Very quickly you are likely to find yourself walking through unfamiliar streets, never-seen-before alleyways, and aspects of the city you never realized were so close to home.

WATERWAYS

◆

My own walks in London tended to follow waterways. I lived for thirty years in Hammersmith, not far from the river. Walks took me upstream or downstream by the Thames, winter or summer, rain or shine; always beginning at my own front door.

THE THAMES CHANGES DAILY with the tides, flooding the towpath beneath the poplars and willows, or revealing muddy gravel beds at low water: always busy with tourist ferries, rowing boats, sailing boats, energetic individuals sculling, or teams pulling in eights, encouraged loudly by their coaches alongside. As you walk, joggers may pass by (some intense, red-faced, and oblivious to the river, looking as though the exercise is doing them more harm than good!), and cyclists will tinkle their bells at the last minute, making you jump. But the river path is a great place for appreciating nature at its best and most beautiful. The light on the Thames is wonderfully and infinitely variable, from cold, grey and choppy, to ice blue, or pink, mauve and flame at sunset; a rich fluid spectrum of living colour. The flowing river is a balm to the mind.

Urban Towpaths

A river enhances a city tremendously. A canal system does the same and presents another ideal opportunity for an urban walk. Like the Thames, the canals have great towpaths and

easy, level walking. Surprisingly, you meet few people, as though the canal were secret; and yet the canals of London run through the most populated areas. The towpath is flat and broad, wide enough for a horse from the days when they towed barges from lock to lock.

My own aim was to use the canals to walk radially to the fringes of London, and I managed to do so in several directions to beyond the M25 orbital road. It is pleasing now to drive this motorway and recollect the canals that inhabit a totally different world beneath the carriageway. Banks of buddleia, hawthorn and dog rose overflow onto the towpath, swans glide by quietly, while the owners of long boats laze on the bank by their moorings. It is all so different from the roaring traffic above.

I walked along these canal towpaths in stages, completing a section at a time. So, for example, I got up early one day and walked out to Uxbridge to have lunch with my daughter Natasha, who worked in an office there; I followed the Thames as far as Kew then turned up the Grand Union canal to Uxbridge. It was spring and the canal path was edged with a rich tapestry of flowers – some wild, some exotic escapees from neighbouring gardens. A kingfisher flew ahead of me part of the way, a flash of electric blue darting along the canal to a new low perch over the water. I picked up a couple of iced buns from an early opening bread shop in Brentford, to keep up my energy levels. Nineteen miles, to a regular foot-beat, in time for lunch at one o'clock. I have to admit it was hard to stand up after steak and chips at the pub, and Natasha had to walk her stiff-legged dad to the station to catch the tube back to Hammersmith!

A week later I took the tube back out to Uxbridge, enjoyed breakfast with my daughter, and walked the Grand Union Canal up to Watford; a week after that completing the next section from Watford to Hemel Hempstead, smiling contentedly as I walked beneath the M25 and quickly left the heavy hum of traffic behind me.

Countryside in the City

The canals have so much to offer the walker. They are as rich in an abundance of birds, flowers, trees or butterflies as anywhere in the countryside. And yet they cut right through the city and some of its most romantic parts. In London you can walk around the north of Regent's Park and the zoo, or through the dockland at Limehouse; through Camden market or behind warm-smelling bread bakeries where rosebay willowherb runs riot along the embankment. Allotments back on to the canal in many places, each a small, tidy world of its own, where people delight in the outdoors and in growing their own fresh produce.

Wherever a road crosses the canal there is almost invariably a pub; and the walker is never far from a transport system: you can get home in no time at all.

RACE & RELIGION – A CULTURAL MIX

◆

Some of the great pleasures of walking, particularly in cities, are the chance encounters with other people. 'Don't ask him, love – he's from Bermondsey!' jibbed the landlady, to much laughter in the pub, when I was once asking directions back to the river.

THERE ARE NO COMPLICATIONS, no expectations; you don't exchange phone numbers or even names, just the pleasure of talking briefly to another human being.

We are all foreigners in the colourful racial mix of the modern city, something worth celebrating and enjoying – the different languages, customs, beliefs and facial features.

When Hebrew nomads, almost four thousand years ago, wandered into the great city of Babel (near present-day Baghdad), they marvelled at its towering ziggurat, and were shocked by the variety of different languages. They concluded that God must have cursed the city. But now we can see this racial mixture as a potential blessing, a gift.

We know the worst – the slums, the squalor, the degradation and poverty (we have read our Dickens; seen the bustees of Mumbai, the shanty towns of Nairobi). We have also experienced the best, the rich life and the tremendous potential. Human culture is a group activity; we are social animals. The best in us emerges when we work together. We should walk along with open eyes, mindful of all its rich possibilities.

THE SPIRITUAL MELTING POT

◆

Mosques, synagogues, churches, temples — they stand cheek by jowl in a city. What can we conclude about religious truth, when there are so many contradictory traditions rubbing shoulders? Some atheists take the view that this proves that they must all be wrong, and that a person's beliefs have less to do with truth than with where they were born. Children born in Ireland will probably become Roman Catholic; those born in Saudi Arabia will become Muslim. They then bring their faiths with them when they migrate to the city.

OF COURSE THE GEOGRAPHICAL OBSERVATION is true, but the atheist conclusion, to my mind, is naive. Religious belief systems illustrate our human desire to make sense of who we are and why we are here. They are culturally diverse attempts to put into words half-grasped insights into our condition. At one level they may contradict each other. Yet at a deeper level they are trying to elucidate our value and our place, and come from the same searching source within. They each shine with a fragment of truth. And the opposite of a profound truth does not have to be a falsehood — it may be another (apparently contradictory) profound truth. Far from proving atheism, the religious differences we find as we walk through the modern city reinforce the importance of religious belief. They raise the wonderful possibility that we might in time find a common language of faith.

ON TREATING A NEW CITY
LIKE A MOUNTAIN RANGE

◆

If presented with a short time in a new city, the walker would do
well to treat it as an unexplored mountain range (using the occa-
sional taxi to bridge the gap between interesting areas). With boots,
rucksack, map and water, you can set off with a few architectural
peaks in mind.

I EXPLORED BEIJING in this way in the 1990s. A cheap pack-
age tour got me to the city and then, rejecting the various
organized group trips on offer, I walked as much as was fea-
sible. Three personal contacts gave my visit a good shape,
goals that provided me with companionship at the end of a
day's tramping. I was immediately struck by the enormous
variety of races I encountered in the streets, races that we
in the west tend in an unthinking way to lump together as
'Chinese'. In fact, my original prejudiced image of a Chinese
face quickly dissolved and has never been replaced.

It was surprising to find a major Confucian temple in a
poor state of repair (it may be different now). All my reading
had given Confucius a high place in Chinese culture and I
imagined that, despite the communism of Mao, he might still
be revered, particularly as he hardly ever mentioned religious
matters in his teachings. But weeds had invaded the marble
steps and stacks of tombstones lay against a wall. It all felt

ill-kempt. Poor Confucius was part of the old order of a fixed society with an unchanging, emperor-dominated hierarchy; he was clearly not the political flavour of the month.

The state of repair of the Confucian temple was very different from the gleamingly new and smartly painted Tibetan Buddhist temple I visited the same day, clean and full of tourists. Surely a communist system could not be publically commending Buddhism? The tourists, of course, were the key. The authorities were keen to present Tibet to the Beijing visitor as a proudly owned part of China.

An Astronomical Treasure

A particular goal I had in mind was the ancient astronomical observatory in Beijing. All my adult life I have lectured in astronomy to groups like the Workers' Educational Association, or classes at St Paul's Girls' School. To be able to visit this old observatory had the nature for me of a small pilgrimage. The site was quite a long way from my hotel but in true pilgrim style I decided to slog my way through the city on foot. Traffic pollution was a problem (it may be better now since the clean-up for the Olympics) so my walk was exhausting and a bit like walking round the London North Circular road in rush hour. People still cycled then, despite the congestion of noxious cars, waves of workers peddling furiously.

The goal made it all worth it. The Chinese are famous for their early astronomical work and here was an observatory

founded in the 15th century in the Ming dynasty. The eight bronze instruments, each taller than a man, date from the Qing dynasty in the 17th century. They stand on a squat tower in the open beneath the grey, polluted Beijing sky, beautifully calibrated with a patina of tarnish – a mix of oriental crafts-manship and western science. Bronze dragons support the meticulous measuring instruments inspired by Jesuit teach-ing. It was inspiring to see the evidence of two different cultures working together in a common quest to understand our complex universe.

I got chased out of the observatory for staying beyond the 40 minutes allocated, despite being the only person there!

LONELINESS & THE CITY WALKER

◆

People have different reasons for being out on the streets, each indi-vidual carrying their own world. I have mentioned Kierkegaard, who needed the energy and distractions of the city from which to draw his thinking; and Dickens, who was driven onto the London pavements to let off his 'superfluous steam'.

SOME PEOPLE ARE LONELY; as you walk through the city people-watching, you can see it in their faces, a sort of tired emptiness and hopelessness. It is an irony, but under-standable, that where people are crammed together at their closest, loneliness can be at its worst. A demographic map of loneliness would always show the concentrations in the cities and not just because there are more people there. Cities can suck the life out of some humans.

Loneliness may sometimes afflict the walker, and it has to be faced. We carry our own worlds with us as we walk; and in those private worlds, we carry our own personal baggage of worries, anxieties or senses of failure. A thought, a recollection or even just a fall in sugar levels may plunge us into despair, and a cold grey cloud passes in front of the sun of our happiness. 'What am I doing here, all on my own, tramping this bit of godforsaken road – how sad is that?' We are gutted.

So long as these feelings of loneliness are part of the normal spectrum of human melancholy, they will pass; it can be interesting to observe the dark cloud as it drifts by, learning a bit of detachment from our feelings, observing them as we might observe the weather. This is in itself part of the practice of mindfulness, part of learning what it means to be human. It can be very satisfying to discover that one can indeed walk through sadness and out of it.

Exchanging Loneliness for Solitariness

Feelings of loneliness have to be addressed, however, in the wider context of everyday life, and not only by observing them mindfully while walking. Personally, I rely very much at such times on thoughts of all the people who are close to me:

THE JOURNALS OF KIERKEGAARD 1834–1854

ALEXANDER DRU (ED. & TRANS.)

FONTANA BOOKS

As a student, I was very influenced by the philosophy of existentialism and Kierkegaard was one of my heroes. A solitary eccentric, he needed the crowds and distractions of the city of Copenhagen to meditate on human nature and faith, valuing chance encounters with other people in the way a botanist might value the discovery of a new plant. This extraordinary 19th-century Christian thinker once wrote, 'Every day I walk myself into a state of well-being and walk away from every illness; I have walked myself into my best thoughts, and I know of no thought so burdensome that one cannot walk away from it....' He once observed, 'What is so confusing about us is that we are at once the Pharisee and the publican.' One of his greatest literary creations, inspired by that noisy think tank, the city, was the Knight of Faith, the person who can make the absurd leap into faith from within the trammels of a conventional life. Kierkegaard contributed greatly to my own reflections on what it means to be a human being.

family and friends. Specifically I think about the person I have arranged to meet that night or the supper invitation I have for the next day. 'Don't be scared of being on your own,' a good friend advised me years ago when I had just separated from my wife. It was the best advice I could have been given.

Having, with divorce, more time on my own, I made a conscious effort to build up a network of friends; people I could meet for a drink or invite for a meal, friends for walks and friends for going to the cinema or art gallery. Within my family I made sure to spend more time individually with my four children and siblings. The benefits were wonderful and I was able as a consequence to rediscover, without fear, the pleasures enjoyed in youth of being solitary. And that solitariness, not the loneliness, is one of the things I love so much about walking on my own.

ON THE NEED TO BE ALERT
TO OTHER PEOPLE & BE SENSIBLE

There are times, when carried away in a private reverie while city walking, that one can forget the need to be careful and properly alert to other people. I missed the signs in Sydney, Australia.

IT WAS ON MY FIRST VISIT TO AUSTRALIA. For a month I enjoyed the use of a flat in Edgecliff, above Double Bay, in exchange for teaching some lessons at Ascham School. It was a perfect arrangement, giving me time to explore the city on foot.

On this occasion, I was walking around part of the south side of Sydney Harbour with my binoculars, finding new flora and fauna everywhere. You could spend a lifetime walking

here. The harbour is a giant fractal inlet from the Pacific
Ocean with a scalloped shoreline of richly treed parks and
wild bush; yacht clubs and expensive bays; rocky promonto-
ries and sandy beaches. Almost every street in Sydney has its
own unique view of the harbour. I had been for a swim on the
Pacific side of the promontory at Bondi, and was now walking
on the less populated inland side facing Shark Island in Sydney
Harbour. A distant glimpse through some bush had suggested
the bobbing shape of a small blue penguin a few yards from
shore. My first penguin ever! Thrill; breathless excitement.

I burst through the bush, ignoring the farmyard squawks of
wattlebirds, the scattering of honeyeaters, and strode out on
to the beach. Sure enough, pulling the binocular image into
focus, there it was, never seen in northern waters – a penguin. I breathed a sigh of pleasure and satisfaction. Lowering
my binoculars, I found myself on a nudist beach.

What do you do with binoculars on a nudist beach? Hide
them and you look guilty. Use them and you look guilty. I
rapidly returned to the bush to investigate the wattlebirds.

The Tale of the Sniper

I had a different experience of not being alert enough to the
people around me when city walking in America. I was visiting friends who worked for the World Bank in Washington.
Kulsum had been a pupil at St Paul's (an ideal student who, a
Muslim, got the highest grades in the class from me for her

essays on St Luke's gospel and later had to be stopped when doing her project on Hinduism when I could see it was becoming impossibly long and I would have to mark it!). They lived in a leafy suburb on the fringes of the Potomac River upstream from the city centre, and gave me a key to their house so that I could come and go as I pleased while they were at work in town.

'Be careful,' they warned; 'keep an eye out for the sniper.'

The whole state was suffering group paranoia at the time. A gunman (who later turned out to be not a terrorist, but an unhappy war veteran from the first Bush invasion of Iraq) was randomly shooting citizens. He even seemed to make a practice of varying his choice of victim. With no pattern to go on, the police were baffled.

I set off for a walk through the neighbourhood, carrying my binoculars. Sniper or no sniper, I wasn't going to be put off the opportunity to spot some North American birds I had not seen before. I reckoned my chances of being shot as negligible – equivalent to being run over by a taxi in London. I gave no thought to other people who lived in the area.

Detached houses sat in their own spacious plots, with large trees and lawns that ran down to the road and no fences – typically American. Not a gated community, but with all the signs of security and neighbourhood watchfulness that sometimes go with wealth in the residential parts of a city. A rich dormitory for city workers.

Cities, as I have often observed, are great havens for wild-life. This was no less true for Washington. I had already seen a pileated woodpecker high on a trunk by the Potomac — a magnificent bird, black as a cleric, with a powerful hammer head and a flamboyant scarlet crest. But now I was listening to a more humble bird, the mockingbird. This mimic thrush has the most gorgeous song, which is celebrated with aching beauty in Walt Whitman's poem, *Sea-Drift*, a sad tale that brings tears to the eyes:

> *Out of the cradle endlessly rocking,*
> *Out of the mockingbird's throat the musical shuttle,*
> *Out of the ninth month midnight, ...*

Now for the first time I could listen to that liquid song, enthralled, not noticing the cars slow down as they drove by.

A car stopped. The window wound down an inch and I was subjected to some sharp questioning from a clearly nervous female driver. What was I doing in the neighbourhood? Why was I carrying binoculars? Why was I walking, not driving? Her foot was poised above the accelerator just in case I turned out to be the sniper.

I tried to set her mind at rest by pointing to the mocking-bird, perched on a tree across the road. She would have none of it. So I decided to prove I was genuine by returning to my friend's home, which was close by. It was only when I tried the key in the lock that I realized I had come to the wrong house.

CHAPTER FOUR

THE DAILY WALK

*The great gift of walking is that it gives
us time to think, letting thoughts and ideas
develop at their own speed, at a natural bodily pace.
Whether the walk is short or long, it gives us an
uninterrupted opportunity to tease things out,
getting a new perspective on a problem. We can
reflect on our experiences, good or bad, get
them into proportion, cast them into the
form of a story; see the funny side.*

AN EVENING WALK

It can be easier to break a habit than it is to establish one. We may sometimes feel lazy and reluctant to bother with the daily walk, especially if the weather is uninviting, wet, windy or cold; but it always turns out to be worth the effort. We can be encouraged by the thought that walking is arguably the best way to keep fit, good for the lungs and the heart.

'I NEED SOME AIR — GOT TO GET OUT!' Most of us have said that, or thought it, at one time or another. There is good reason to take a walk in the evening. We all know that feeling of having been cooped up all day at home or in the office, trapped, suffering cabin fever, stuck inside and stiff-shouldered from desk work. Walking opens the lungs to fresh air, gets the heart pumping, exercises the body and helps to put the day behind us. Even God in the poetry of the Bible takes a walk in the Garden of Eden 'in the cool of the evening'.

In town or country, for 15 minutes or an hour, an evening walk has always been part of my life. Now that I live in East Sussex, the South Downs are an obvious attraction. After five minutes' walk from our home in Alfriston I am following a lane between high hedges that takes me to the north-facing foot of the Downs, where I follow a path for half a mile in the direction of Firle. In winter this track lies in the shadow of the hill so I am always eager to cut up diagonally onto the tops,

to be greeted by the wind and great views down to the sea.

I am coming across some lovely new words and phrases: where a track cuts deep into the landscape – a 'holloway'; where generations of ploughing has begun to form terraces – 'plough drift'.

BETWEEN THE WOODS & THE WATER

PATRICK LEIGH FERMOR
PENGUIN BOOKS, ISBN 0-14-009430-X

I dipped into this travel book years ago on the recommendation of a colleague and was immediately hooked; the best of its genre I have ever read. Leigh Fermor, at the age of 18, walked from Holland to Constantinople, starting in 1934, and experienced Europe just before it was convulsed by war and changed for ever. He describes those parts of his journey that lie between the woods of Transylvania and the waters of the Danube. It is pure magic. Strolling from castle to castle, he crosses the Great Hungarian Plain and receives wonderful hospitality; he also sleeps in ditches and haystacks; watches hares by moonlight and is struck by the colours of birds not seen before – orioles and bee-eaters. He has a tremendous eye for detail, both of nature and of the people he encounters. In the passage that first grabbed me, he tells how he slept beneath the stars on a ledge in the Carpathian Mountains. At dawn he finds himself transfixed as he observes a golden eagle preening itself only metres away. It is a book to return to.

ENJOYING THE SEASONS

◆

One of the great delights of a familiar short walk is noting the changing of the seasons; absorbing what you see. Sometimes at the end of a day one can be over-preoccupied with unsettled thoughts, with gaze vaguely fixed on the path at one's feet.

I MINDFULLY REMIND MYSELF TO LIFT MY HEAD and make a point of looking up at the horizon. Thinking is no more difficult with your head up! That way I do not miss the green woodpecker fly up from the verge; a kestrel, the 'standing hawk', hovering motionless above a patch of rough grass; cloud shadows drifting across a cornfield.

I am currently teaching myself to identify Downland butterflies. 'Learning the names is a method of noticing,' observes William Fiennes in his lovely book *The Snow Geese*. He is right. To identify a butterfly you have to pursue it and look closely at the details and in doing so you begin to appreciate its beauty. I had never realized that the *underside* of a butterfly's wing could be so intricately gorgeous.

The Comfort of Familiar Sights and Sounds

When you know the path well you begin to look for familiar friends. There is a family of stonechats that flit along the fence at the foot of the Downs, winter and summer. In the spring they are joined by nesting whitethroats, blackcaps, and willow warblers with their delicious trickle of song. In early spring, and then again in autumn, their numbers are swollen by wonderfully coloured wheatears (grey, apricot and black with a white rump – their original name being 'white-arse'), which I associate with the stone walls and fells of Cumbria.

Wheatears make a long migratory journey annually from south of the Sahara. I have seen them in Kenya, looking as completely at home perched on elephant dung as they do on a drystone wall in Wasdale. They stop off on the Downs, in the spring, to recover their energy before flying on to mountainous districts in the north of the UK – or even to Iceland. In the autumn they rest here again to put on some weight before crossing the channel and on back to the African savannah. Is the wheatear an African bird nesting in England, or an English bird wintering in Africa?

The Frothing of Spring

In spring, the angelica froths bright green along the banks of the lane and violets are tucked away in the shadows; I shove my nose into a bunch and inhale the delicate scent. Sometimes there are white ones among them. Once I accidently discovered a robin's nest tucked away between the new growth and the old ivy. Little eyes peered questioningly at me as I cautiously walked past day after day.

In early summer there are carpets of cowslips nodding in the breeze, with a subtle scent that takes me back to my

earliest childhood. I look for orchids; the early purple orchid and the pyramidal orchid grow in their thousands on the chalk of the Downs, deep purple and beautiful; occasionally I find an exotic bee orchid hiding in the long dry grass. Sometimes I make a detour, when walking this way in summer, to a steep bank where there are patches of wild pinks (are they escapees or naturally wild, I wonder?). Their strong heavy scent of cloves brings me to my knees.

The Days Shorten

One autumn, with the days growing cooler, a thousand swallows gathered twittering in a newly ploughed field, waiting for the right wind to carry them south across the English Channel; next day they were gone. It is at about that time that I look out every year for a particular ironwood tree, whose leaves begin to turn the deep purple of haematite; and for an ash that for some unaccountable reason turns pure yellow well before the others.

Winter comes on fast, and the setting point of the sun moves south along the horizon of France Hill. Standing by the same field gate, I can plot its course week by week until in late December it stops its movement south and stands still at the winter solstice. This was how our ancestors kept track of the seasons, marking them by standing stones and henges, creating the first calendars. Stonehenge is built on such a plan and also many other stone circles and Neolithic burial chambers.

THE NARROW ROAD TO THE DEEP NORTH & OTHER TRAVEL SKETCHES

MATSUO BASHO, TRANS. NOBUYUKI YUASA
PENGUIN BOOKS, ISBN 0-14-044-185-9

This 17th-century classic of Japanese literature introduced me to the spare and elegant form of the 17-syllable haiku. Basho, the greatest of the Japanese Haiku poets, spent years wandering the roads of Japan. I imagine him like one of those little figures that appear in Zen landscape art, dwarfed by mountains and mists. He was a free spirit observing the tiny details of nature with an amused eye, a mystic roaming through the natural world. Influenced by Zen Buddhism, his travel sketches record in prose and poetry his recurring discovery of the eternal in the ephemeral, finding beauty in the ordinary, capturing a moment in a few words. I am reminded on rereading him of how William Blake could see 'A world in a grain of sand, And a heaven in a wild flower'. Here in translation is one of his haikus:

A thicket of summer grass
Is all that remains
Of the dreams and ambitions
Of ancient warriors.

KEEPING A JOURNAL

◆

I find that it is worth keeping a journal. It is not a strict affair and I only use it, an A4-sized notebook, to jot down a new thought, or a description of something I have seen; occasionally a rough sketch, an idea for a painting. Weeks pass and it remains untouched; but it is always there in case I want to record something.

A BRIEF NOTE IMPROVES THE MEMORY; the anticipation of writing something down actually enhances the observation. I even venture sometimes to turn an experience into a haiku; I find it focuses the mind. The haiku is the most austere of poetry forms and was invented within the Japanese Zen tradition. The poem contains just 17 syllables.

I am not a purist, and so do not always manage to achieve the traditional 5-7-5 pattern. But that does not matter because I only write them for my own satisfaction – and to distil an experience into as few words as possible. I will risk giving a couple of examples here.

The first is from an early winter walk when the old man's beard is at its whitest and most fluffy as it scrambles over the hawthorn and sloe. I was struck one evening by the way it shone with the sun behind it:

> *The low winter sun*
> *Burning cold, fires with glory*
> *Tufts of old man's beard.*

Another comes from a walk down a hillside in Cumbria, also in winter and after a low cloud had soaked the valley; a wet bare-limbed tree sparkled with colours from all over the spectrum as the sun burst through a patch of torn cloud:

> *Scintillating gems*
> *Emerald dewdrops flash ruby*
> *On the mountain ash.*

If I hadn't written the haikus I might well have forgotten the essence of those moments.

REFLECTIONS ON FORGIVENESS & MINDFULNESS

◆

Sometimes we carry a burden on the evening walk; a hurt, anger, or perhaps an unhappy recollection of a conversation we replay over and over again, thinking of what we should have said or could have said. An annoying incident experienced during the day can fester.

THE END OF THE DAY IS THE TIME to let these things go. Drop it! The Buddha's advice is to note these thoughts, face them and acknowledge them – and *then* dismiss them. With practice this will work for most irritating interruptions to our peaceful walk.

Just for a moment, stand still. Be aware of your breathing, the breath flowing in and the breath flowing out. Don't force it. Don't hyperventilate. Don't pant. Just gently open your shoulders, let your back unwind a little and straighten. Feel the air flow naturally deep into your lungs (don't force it); hold it for a moment while it is comfortable; then let it flow out again. This exercise, 'coming back to your body', can be very comforting. There is healing in your own breath.

Then start walking. Find your own pace; don't rush. Let a gentle rhythm develop between your walking and breathing; be aware of each step and each breath. *Let go of thinking.*

In this way you can leave behind the bad business of the day, simply 'walk it off'.

But sometimes this is easier said than done. What of the deep hurt that has been with us for a long time – maybe years? How do we handle that? The thought can become a poisonous feeling, sickening the body; turn away from it and there it is; think of something else and like a bully it elbows its way back, demanding your attention.

The walking can still help. Be *mindful* of walking. When walking – just walk. One day you will wake to the discovery that these hurtful thoughts are *not you*, no more than are the black clouds on a rainy day. But meanwhile they can cause great pain; invasive seeds that have taken root in your mind and body, becoming part of your 'hard drive'. Parasitic, they take hold and *become* you.

The Buddhist Path

Buddhist teaching has a lot to say about how to handle one's difficult feelings. This is perhaps one of the reasons why the tradition is becoming increasingly popular in the west, where the pressures of the modern day-to-day prove too much for some. Many people find the writings of the Vietnamese monk Thich Nhat Hanh helpful. This Zen master has the blessing of the Dalai Lama.

Don't be put off by the monk's style – it is very simple and some readers may find it too sweet and even at first rather cloying (the repetitive instructions to smile, for example). It is worth persevering, however, and much deep wisdom will be found; *The Miracle of Mindfulness* and *Peace is Every Step* are both worth reading for his thoughts on how to prevent the seeds of anger from taking root in our being.

Nhat Hanh's simple but profound message is that happiness and peace can always be found in the present moment – indeed only in the present moment. 'The well is within us, and if we dig deeply in the present moment, the water will spring forth. We must go back to the present moment to be really alive.' The sound of a bell in a Zen Buddhist monastery brings the monk back to his true self. Nhat Hanh gives advice on how we can return to our true selves among the distractions of the modern world – a red traffic light can be used as an instrument of mindfulness in the same way; or the ring-tone of a telephone.

The Christian Way

The Christian tradition teaches that forgiveness is the solution but often without elaborating on how to go about it. Jesus said that it is not enough to love our family and friends, we should also love our enemies – remembering, of course, that the hurt we struggle to forgive may well have been inflicted by someone very close to us, in which case they become the 'enemy' we should love and forgive.

I sometimes feel uneasy with the way the concept of forgiveness is presented. It suggests a certain condescension from the moral high ground, reinforced by that popular phrase 'I'll forgive – but I'll never forget'. And I wonder whether Jesus meant it to be a command at all. Perhaps he was just offering some good news: 'Yes – it is possible to forgive – and forget.' Both people benefit – the forgiven and the forgiver. What a relief it can be to find that to be true!

So practising forgiveness is actually a practice of mindfulness, an exercise in letting go, in the way we manage to overcome the small irritations of the day when we set out for the evening walk. Buddhism and Christianity can both help us in this. After all, some day, when we die, we are going to have to let go of everything. So why not let go some of it now – particularly if it is a pain? What a waste of time not to.

WALKING WITH SELF-GUILT

◆

A bigger problem when taking the daily walk is sometimes harder to recognize: harder to recognize because it is so obvious. Self-blame. Guilty feelings. We are so sure that we have let ourselves down, or let someone else down, that we forget to question our burden of self-blame and just feel miserable.

WE FEEL A USELESS PERSON, a waste of space; we feel weighed down. We may even be in danger of indulging feelings of self-hate.

Mindfulness can help. When I feel horribly guilty and low about myself, I have to remember that I am after all only a person living in the here and now. It can be difficult being a human being, we all know that. But this should never become an excuse. It is then that I really have to learn to forgive, and accept myself for being the way I am and move on. Feelings of guilt are the nudge we need to change our ways, *do* something about the issue at hand that has caused the self-loathing, *act* with positive compassion, *say sorry* or whatever; but then move on. Let go of the guilt.

The Zen-like Simplicity of Jesus' Teaching

I am afraid that my own religious tradition has wandered wildly off course in matters of guilt. It has built a whole edifice on feelings of being a miserable sinner. A sort of negative

self-indulgence has been encouraged. It became the great sales pitch for launching Jesus as the solution. He died for our sins. God sent him, his only Son, into the world to take the punishment for our guilt, the Original Sin we are all supposed to inherit from Adam and Eve in the Garden of Eden. The crucifixion is offered as a focus for our gratitude to God.

I cannot value – or even understand – such an idea of God.

Jesus' message is almost Zen-like in its simplicity – the Kingdom of God is close at hand, within us and among us. His teaching is a distillation of the Jewish Torah – 'Love God and Love your neighbour as yourself.' And nothing could be more straightforward than his guidance on prayer – the Lord's Prayer. He was murdered by the Romans for political reasons.

When, finally, I mindfully get my feelings of self-guilt in proportion while walking, it is like suddenly waking up and breathing in fresh air. Once more I notice the flowers in the passing hedgerow, the untidy badger set in the bank of the holloway, the clouds signalling a change in the weather. Life is good again.

FIELD WALKING

◆

A pastime that gives me great pleasure is field walking, to find what has been turned up by the plough. Times spent in Gloucestershire, with the permission of friendly farmers, have always been rewarding and I have a cherished collection of stones used for grinding wheat or sharpening scythes, and flint arrowheads dropped long before Jesus walked in the Judean hills.

FIELD WALKING TAKES TIME AND PATIENCE and is not for all the family! It must be like fishing; it either grabs you as an activity or it doesn't.

The great thing about searching for pieces of 'worked' flint in the Cotswolds is that there is no natural flint in the ground, unlike where I live now in East Sussex. Here on the South Downs, *all* of the loose stones are flint and have been freed from the chalk by weathering, sheep foot or plough. When walking on a shoulder of the Downs where the flint has been exposed, I have a problem following my own advice to keep my head up and be aware of all that is around me! I sweep my eyes over the flints, totally riveted by their extraordinary shapes, hollows and holes, some looking like pieces of sculpture by Henry Moore or Barbara Hepworth.

But in Gloucestershire, all the stone lying on the surface of a ploughed field is the local honey-coloured oolitic limestone, sometimes containing fossilized clamshells or sea urchins.

Any flint has to have been imported from the Marlborough Downs in Wiltshire, the nearest source.

Murmurs from the Stone Age

After the plough there has to be rain and then the white oxidized flint stands out clearly. I am still exhilarated by catching sight of an edge of flint poking up through the turned sod. It might be nothing special – a discarded flake, perhaps, or, more interesting, a core from which flakes have been knapped to make the pieces to be used for fashioning arrowheads.

Hours of slow walking, eyes fixed a few feet ahead, may then be rewarded with a beautifully worked arrowhead, or a curved scrapper for cleaning leather. Once I found half of a broken axe head, and another time a chunk of bronze from the Bronze Age. I don't use a metal detector because it is stones that fascinate me (though I have come across Roman nails and a Roman coin dated by the local museum as having been minted in Arles in AD 346).

It is particularly satisfying to find a stone tool, a hand-sized lump of, perhaps, quartzite, imported and prized for its hardness. The telltale signs are its foreignness in a field of limestone, and the way that one edge has been worn smooth from hours of grinding corn or knapping flints. The most exciting characteristic is the way it fits in the hand comfortably, giving one an almost instant rapport with the hand that last dropped it, perhaps five thousand years ago.

A Family Link with the Land

On one occasion, over thirty years ago, I spent an afternoon pacing up and down a particularly fruitful field with my youngest son Josh. He was about nine months old at the time and I carried him burbling on my back. Finally he fell asleep and so I very gently laid him in a plough furrow at the centre of the field and resumed my quartering of the land. I kept looking back at the quiet bundle and managed a whole hour of flint-searching before I saw a little leg kick the air and quickly retrieved him.

Years later Josh founded a summer music festival in the Winterwell Valley, just below the field. I like to think that his sleep in the furrow established a link with this bit of land!

Now, every year, most of the family manage to congregate at Winterwell (with hundreds of others) for a wonderful weekend of food, drink, music and a chance to catch up gossip at its best.

CHAPTER FIVE

THE WALK TO WORK

There is something special about walking to work with the whole day ahead. It makes creative use of a journey you have to make anyway — and there is no argument about when to do it; it dictates its own time. The walking brings the body alive after sleep and provides a wonderful opportunity to clear the head and quietly sort out the day's tasks mindfully, without interruptions from other people.

NECESSITY'S NUDGE

◆

The first experience of walking to work may have been out of necessity — the buses not running, a snowstorm, or maybe just a flat tyre on your usually reliable bike. Whatever it was could be seen, in retrospect, as a blessing in disguise.

I WAS VISITING NEW YORK IN 1980, staying in the Upper East Side on Lexington, when there was a transit strike — the whole subway network was closed down for weeks. The morning's usual cramped rush hour on the underground was replaced by waves of walkers making their way down Manhattan, block by block, to get to their offices in the city. Bankers bound for Wall Street wove down Fifth Avenue on roller skates with a new-found freedom.

It was wonderful. The city had discovered the benefits of walking to work. No doubt it came as a shock and hardship for some; but many continued to walk after the transit dispute was resolved.

Nat's Walk to Work

All my life I have lived just round the corner from my workplace and so my first-hand experience of walking to work is pretty limited — I am dependent on conversations with my son Nat. He worked for a couple of years at what seemed to me to be a highly stressful job selling training in an IT company

just off Oxford Street. He lived in a flat by the Thames in Chiswick and the normal method for getting to work would be to brave the claustrophobic crush of the tube to Oxford Circus or the slow toil of commuters on a bus running up Notting Hill and through Bayswater. He decided to walk.

His daily route (which had plenty of scope for variation day by day) usually took him along the Thames Embankment, where the wind blows fresh, the tide is ever changing, and the gulls, geese and crows enjoy their morning on the mud. Cormorants dive and emerge with eels writhing around their beaks as they attempt, and then manage, to swallow them.

After a zigzag through Hammersmith he walked through Holland Park, notorious for its noisy peacocks and lazy foxes. From there he strode on to Kensington Gardens with the skyline of London all around but low and beyond the trees. Crossing the Serpentine, he walked through the wide expanse of Hyde Park and into Oxford Street. The four miles took an hour, not much longer than it takes by bus.

Nat arrived at work clear-headed and exercised, heart pumping and lungs wide open; London, with its changing weather and seasons, was his own personal territory. An added advantage, he tells me, is that once you know your route you can time your arrival accurately – unlike the unpredictability of the rush-hour traffic. 'Leave three minutes late and you arrive three minutes late – leave twenty minutes early and you know for sure that you will be early.'

Walking to School Years Ago

Another great advantage of walking to work is that, unlike many exercise routines, it is so easy to organize; you have to get there anyway and the time is already fixed – so why not benefit from the opportunity? Get ahead, even before the work day has begun! And arrive at your desk feeling in control of the day instead of its victim.

It is easy to feel reluctant to set off to walk to work, tempted perhaps to stay half asleep as long as possible on tube or bus – particularly if the morning is dark and damp. But Nat says he always found it was worth it.

I can vouch for this pleasure of getting ahead and feeling fit, because although I have never had a lengthy walk to work, I did walk five miles to school for a year when I was 17. I was preparing for an 8-week exploring holiday in Labrador and needed the exercise. We lived in Somerset and my school was in Minehead. The whole journey by bus from our village to a connecting bus on the main road took almost an hour. By leaving home only 20 minutes earlier I arrived at school at the same time as everyone else.

Fortunately for me, my quickest walking route followed a track over a shoulder of Exmoor, through magnificent scenery. The initial climb was stiff and very good exercise for the calves. Some autumn mornings it took me through a blanket of mist to emerge minutes later into brilliant sunshine and a blue sky. A white sea of cloud now lay below me, hiding the

valleys and turning other shoulders of Exmoor into low islands in an ocean of cotton wool. In winter, wading through snow gave an additional exhilarating challenge – and was even tougher on the legs.

The path cut through some heathland and pinewoods. Distant views of southern Wales across the Severn Estuary presented themselves before the track curved down towards Minehead. The occasional red deer looked a bit startled before rapidly disappearing – clearly not expecting to share his territory at that hour of the morning. These moments became secret remembered pleasures as I sat through physics and maths lessons later in the day.

OPPORTUNITIES FOR PRAYER

It was doing this regular morning walk that gave me a new idea about prayer. Saying prayers as a child was something one did before getting into bed, a simple but good habit, I believe.

THE SUBJECT CAME UP IN CONVERSATION one evening with my mother. She asked how my morning walk had been; 'Any more deer?'

'It's odd,' I said, 'There's a chap at school – I hardly know him and can't say whether I like him or dislike him; but I found myself thinking about him recently when I was walking to school. I don't know why. It was when I was walking through a patch of heather right up on the tops. Now, every time I pass that spot, he pops into my head. That's what's odd.'

My mother, doing the ironing, thought a moment.

'You know what I think your godfather would say? He'd say it gave you an opportunity to pray for him.'

I don't think I had thought before that praying was something you could do while doing something else.

On another occasion my father told me of a retreat for clergy he had been on years before. A young novice had asked the old retreat master if it was OK if he smoked while he said his prayers. 'Absolutely not!' came the answer. 'But you could try praying while you are smoking – that would be fine.'

Praying for Others

Praying for other people – family, friends or 'enemies' – can only be a good thing. At the very least, by extending feelings of compassion to those around us, we put ourselves in the right frame of mind to relate to them, particularly if we are going to meet them during the day. There can be no better time to do this than during the daily walk to work.

Each day, we face the miracle of *newness* – the hours ahead have never happened before. To be sure, some things are fixed and certain: walking to work in the winter will see us wrapped up in coat and muffler, wondering if the sun will show its face before we get to the office. In spring, bursting buds and fresh

leaves will raise our spirits; the summer will bring heat and we know to dress lightly. All such things as these are expected.

And the day at work itself will have a solid, predictable framework, with predetermined tasks to be faced and people to be handled – we already know from experience those colleagues who are easy to work with and those who have a way of driving us up the wall.

But the activity of walking has its own lesson to teach us as we face the day. It is empowering. Walking is a sort of living symbol for taking the initiative; the body reminds the mind that together they are in control and not passive victims of circumstance. Much of the day ahead will be fixed. But, we should mindfully remind ourselves, we have the miraculous freedom to decide *how to face the day*.

We have freedom to make the decisions we know we should make; to take a stand when we judge it is important to do so, to speak or not to speak. We have the freedom to stand back mindfully from that difficult colleague and refuse to be drawn into a descending spiral of bad feeling. In fact, the more we face the day mindfully, the more we will discover that we are free to act and think in new ways.

So much can be achieved by walking mindfully and prayerfully to work – and by believing that the details of the day are not fixed and predetermined. We can expect the miracle of newness. 'This is the Day the Lord has made,' wrote the psalmist in Psalm 118. 'Let us rejoice and give thanks in it.'

CHAPTER SIX

THE NIGHT WALK

*Few people today have the opportunity, in
our over-illuminated and energy-wasteful world,
truly to know the dark, or to discover how beautiful it
can be to walk on a dark night. I wish there could be
an annual 'Lights off' night when, for an hour
(depending of course on the weather!), children in
cities could experience the wonder of the Milky Way.
The police and motoring organizations would have
their reasonable objections — but I can't think
that they would be insurmountable. And just
think of the energy saved!*

OUR PERCEPTION OF DARKNESS

◆

The dark comes in for a bad press in ancient mythology; the world becomes a battleground between good and evil, light and dark. Sinners perform their shameful 'works of darkness', while the darkness of ignorance clouds the minds of those not yet illuminated.

EVEN THE BIBLE IS INFLUENCED by this mythological language. St Paul writes of Christians as the 'children of light', leaving everyone else to be children of darkness; Jesus is the Light of the World – and we have all heard of the Prince of Darkness. Such mythological language has its useful and proper place; but it can be a good thing to learn to love the real dark.

It was walking home from the pub one night with my brother Inigo and his wife Kerry that we hit on an idea. They live in Cumbria in Wasdale and the rough track home from their local pub is the darkest I know. We find our way by looking up at the sky through overhanging branches; the faint light, reflected, gives warning of puddles ahead. To our left a gurgling stream, Cinder Beck, is a coil of black sound.

'Let's climb Scafell in the dark, one night,' Kerry suggested.

Walking in Moon Shadows

A fortnight later, knowing there would be a full moon, and with minimal preparation, we decided to go for it. Flasks of coffee and a jumper each seemed enough. In summer the moon lies low on the horizon and although it had risen when we set off, it was still hidden by the bulk of the Scafell range.

Even a familiar path takes on an air of strangeness in the dark and the walker orientates himself in a different way — looking for the silhouette of a shoulder of rock, keeping the sound of a stream close by, checking the step ahead, probing the shadows, listening.

THE AUTOBIOGRAPHY OF A SUPER-TRAMP

W H DAVIES (PREFACE BY GEORGE BERNARD SHAW)

JONATHAN CAPE

I have often been caught in the rain when walking, and sheltered beneath a tree, or braved the elements, allowing myself to get soaked with the happy thought of a warm pub not too far away. It is then that I think of travellers who have no comfortable bed awaiting them; the tramps of this world. 'The greatest enemy to the man who has to carry on his body all of his wardrobe, is rain,' records this tramp in an autobiography that is an extraordinary and rare piece of writing. In England he tramps through Devon and Somerset, often soaked to the skin, and finds more generosity among the poor than he does from the rich. In New England he is treated well and has a glorious time walking six miles every day with a friend, along the coast of Connecticut. He is always philosophical.

The night was cool, but the steep climb was just as hard and heat-generating. Jumpers were quickly removed and pushed into rucksacks. We assumed we were alone but then there was a clattering of stones up ahead that we thought at first might be sheep. Out of the shadows emerged a panting party of young men who thundered past us, going downhill. 'The Three Peaks!' they shouted in explanation as they disappeared into the dark. The Three Peaks is a famous challenge for those fit enough to attempt it: Snowdon in North Wales, Ben Nevis in Scotland and Scafell Pike in 24 hours.

The path became treacherous at Hollow Stones with its rubble of rocks dumped in the ice age. The sky ahead was brightening and the stars fading as we awaited our own moonrise. Gothic silhouettes of dark crags loomed ahead, Pikes Crag, Pulpit Rock and Mickledore.

We waited. A burning band of gold appeared on the high horizon and, as we watched, the moon slowly sailed free.

Such moments are irreplaceable and we stood for some time just gazing at the face of the moon with its random pattern of dark smudges.

The Man in the Moon

'What do you see?' I asked.

'A man with a gun and a dog? A hare?'

'You're supposed to see the face of the Man in the Moon,' I suggested, 'but I can never make it out.'

So I told them about my small personal discovery in Australia; that when I had been staying at Uluru I had gone for a night stroll and watched the moon. Of course, in Australia one has to look north to see both the sun and the moon and they travel across the sky from right to left, the opposite to what we experience in the UK; and that, even when it is expected, feels very odd.

But what did surprise me, after a lifetime of trying to see the face of the Man in the Moon, was that suddenly there it was – a broad beaming face smiling down at me! Two big eyes beneath a bald forehead (one eye made up like a clown's), healthy cheeks and a big mouth. Was the face of the Man in the Moon dreamed up by an Aboriginal storyteller?

If another party of 'Three Peaks' hikers had passed at that moment, they would have witnessed a strange ceremony, finding the three of us bending over, bottoms to the sky, to gaze up at the moon between our legs! Seen upside down, the Man in the Moon smiled at me again.

The trek to the top was magnificent, moonlight shining off slabs of bare rock, moon shadows falling into every cleft and under every overhang. On the final peak of Scafell Pike there is a large cairn where one can shelter from the wind, whatever its direction. We had donned our jumpers again when resting at Hollow Stones and now I noticed that Inigo and Kerry had just removed theirs and were rummaging in their rucksacks. I noticed, too, at the same moment, that now I had stopped climbing the sweat on my back and in my vest had turned very cold.

'What are you doing?' I asked.

'Just changing our tee shirts for dry ones,' they answered. 'Didn't you bring one with you?'

A flaming sunrise, an hour and a half later, over Great End; and the coffee steaming from the flask, made me almost forget my foolish oversight.

CONSTELLATIONS IN THE NIGHT SKY

The constellations in the night sky can be a great comfort; whatever happens here on earth they remain the same, swinging slowly across the heavens from east to west as the earth spins daily on its axis.

I GREW TO KNOW THEM WHEN I WAS 12 YEARS OLD and responsible for shutting up the chickens at the end of the garden. 'Vega in the constellation of Lyra the lyre,' I would murmur to myself, thrilled by the name, but still slightly nervous of the dark.

A walk on a clear night with the stars above reveals a new dimension to our lives, opening up a great window on the sky. How can we avoid being affected by this, when even a small amount of knowledge can transform the way we think about ourselves and our place in the universe? It is well worth

finding a place to walk where the light pollution is at a minimum. Once you have found a spot from which you can see the ribbon of the Milky Way and stars near the horizon, then you can smile! The South Downs, I have discovered, can be pretty good for this. My partner Ros and I once took a bottle of wine and walked up on to the Downs on 12th August. It was the night of the annual Perseid meteor shower. We counted more than seventy shooting stars in an hour! We couldn't have done that in London, I think.

A Change of Perspective

If you stand still for a few minutes (and it only takes that time), you can get the feel for yourself that Planet Earth is turning. Line up a bright star (or the moon) with the branch of a tree, or a chimney pot – or watch it in the west, if it is near the horizon. After a few minutes it will have become obvious that it has moved. Then tell yourself, 'No! I didn't move and the star didn't move. It was the earth turning.'

The first time I was able to get this switch of perspective was standing on a hill in north Cumbria watching, mindfully, the constellation of Orion setting over the Irish Sea. What was really happening, of course, was that Cumbria and the Irish Sea were slowly swinging up into the sky, me with them, hiding Orion star by star. We know with our minds that the Earth turns on its axis giving us day and night, but really knowing it as an experience has a totally different feel to it.

DOES THE UNIVERSE
HAVE TO MAKE US FEEL SMALL?

◆

When we walk down a lane at night, beneath trees, the constellations seem to walk with us unchanging, unlike everything else that we pass by. In fact, if we walked in a straight line horizontally for a whole lifetime along an unimaginably long lane, they would continue to seem to be walking with us and wouldn't alter at all.

IT IS THE DISTANCES we find baffling. The light from the moon, a quarter of a million miles away, gets to the eye in one and a quarter seconds. And yet for a close star like Vega, one of the bright stars in the summer triangle, high overhead on an August night, the light takes 26 years to get here. What we see was happening 26 years ago (what were we doing then you might wonder?). Even the moon seems, to us, to be far away – but where does that put Vega in the scale of things? And to add to the sense of wonderment, we now know that our own solar system of sun, moons and planets is drifting slowly, cosmically speaking, towards Vega at 12 miles per second all the time. If you are strolling at three miles an hour and look up at Vega, knowing about that star drift, it can make you feel quite giddy.

The summer triangle of bright stars is made up of Vega in the constellation of Lyra, Deneb in the tail of Cygnus the Swan, and Altair in Aquila the Eagle. Deneb is the furthest –

but still a close neighbour in astronomical terms. A rough calculation reveals that if you had a magic carpet and could fly towards Deneb, instead of going for your night walk, the journey might take longer than you think. Fly at a million miles an hour, every hour, day and night, for a million years and you would still have a little way to go!

It makes us feel distinctly small, as we wander down a lane in the dark.

Are We Nothing Then?

A popular line of argument from some New Atheists is that science has knocked us off our pedestal and revealed that we are no more than a rather complex biological scum on the surface of the Earth. It began with Copernicus, who shifted the planet from the centre of creation and set it in orbit around the sun. Then Charles Darwin upset many Victorians by demonstrating that people are just animals with apes in their family trees. Twentieth-century astrophysics completed our character assassination by revealing that the sun is just an ordinary star; one amongst the billions.

But people are naive if they think that there is only one way to read the facts, or that size is a measure of value.

Looked at another way, the facts about the size and age of the cosmos (vast and ancient — it had to be in order to create the chemistry needed for life), and the evolution of life itself on the planet (miraculous), reveal that the wakefulness of a

> I firmly believe that we misread the Bible if we forget the
> principle of *the inspiration of the reader*. We should read
> scripture in the same way we might have a dialogue with an
> aged and wise relative, showing respect for what they say but
> not feeling that we always have to agree. We can be just as
> inspired in our understanding of who we are and why we are
> here as were those who wrote the Bible. Fundamentalists
> are hooked on the idea that scripture is the unquestionable
> and literal word of God, not recognizing that whatever wise
> insights it contains have been filtered through the fallible,
> racist, sexist, homophobic minds of its writers.

human being is a marvellous and quite extraordinary phe-
nomenon to emerge on the surface of the Earth. Would it be
too much to think of ourselves as at the frontier of evolution,
pioneers in the process of mind being born out of matter? It
is only a negative misreading of the science that gnaws away at
our self-esteem.

The Bible is also much misread.

The Biblical View of Our Value

The unknown author of Psalm 8 is astonished at his own place
in creation. 'For I will consider thy heavens, even the works
of thy fingers: the moon and star which thou hast ordained.

What is man, that thou art mindful of him: and the son of man, that thou visitest him?' A nice thought, as we walk mindfully at night looking up at the stars, that the creator of all of this is mindful of us!

There is no science in the Bible – how could there be? Mankind had not yet started to think in a scientific way when the writings of the Bible were being put together. The creation stories of Genesis are poetry, attempting to reveal some insights into our place and purpose. One insight is that men and women are made in the image of God; that the wakeful human mind, attuned potentially to beauty, compassion and justice, is a mirror of the creative mind that is still creating us.

WALKING WITH THE MOON

As we walk down our lane at night, the moon walks with us, accompanying us past the trees and gateways, sailing along the top of the hedgerows, peaceful and calm.

IT IS AN EASY MATTER TO FIND A MAP of the lunar features and learn some of their names: top right is the *Mare Crisium*, the Sea of Crises; bottom left the *Mare Humorum*, the Sea of Clouds. The large dark area is the Ocean of Storms, while the bright spot near the centre is the giant crater Copernicus, named after the man who dislodged the Earth from its place at the centre of creation. Another bright spot at the hub of a system of radiating rays (also visible to the naked eye) is Tycho, named after Tycho Brahe. This 16th/early 17th-century Danish astronomer provided Kepler with accurate measurements of the positions of the planets, which laid the groundwork for Kepler's discovery of how all planets orbit the sun in ellipses.

With the naked eye you can even see, when you know where to look, the first rays of the sun rising on a great crescent of mountains called the Bay of Rainbows; the peaks stand out like stars in the night, while the floor of the bay is still shrouded in darkness.

Looking Up at the Earth

Contemplating another world while walking can be a wonderful pleasure. On a windy night the moon seems to sail through the clouds, flaring and fading as they race past. And beyond our earthbound clouds, there is the Sea of Clouds and the Sea of Tranquillity. The names are worth knowing.

Change the perspective for a moment and imagine we are walking on the moon looking up at Earth (note: not down!). This is quite easy to do because we have been told what it is like; men have walked there.

I had the great privilege some years ago of walking with the astronaut Dave Scott; he was commander of Apollo 15 and spent time bouncing about with a Lunar Rover at the foot

of the Apennine Mountains by a winding valley called Hadley Rill. He and his colleague collected rock for the geologists and found some of the oldest material known as the 'Genesis rock', as ancient as the solar system itself – four and a half billion years. It was strange to walk next to a man who had walked on the Sea of Rains picking up stones, just as I might pick up flints on the Downs!

An Extraterrestrial Moment of Mindfulness?

Dave Scott had his own moment of mindfulness and was struck by the beauty of the Earth seen from the moon. 'It hangs in the black sky like a glass bauble, a blue and white Christmas tree decoration. It's a small, fragile world.'

This image of a fragile Earth hanging in empty space has become part of the modern psyche. We begin to see how vulnerable we actually are. We are the first generation truly to see this. We are also the generation that is coming closest to polluting and destroying it.

The Bible gives mankind 'dominion' over all other animals. Understandable perhaps at the time of writing, but this is a bit of scripture we need to rethink radically. Our brains are more complex and our minds more awake to the reality around us (at least potentially) than those of other animals, but that gives us no right of dominion. Rather we have a responsibility of care. Protecting the biodiversity of the planet has become a moral imperative of our age.

However we look at it, this has become a compelling truth; whether gazing up at the stars as we walk mindfully at night, or contemplating the Earth from the moon, we face an unavoidable challenge.

DO PEOPLE WALK ON OTHER WORLDS?

◆

People have walked on the moon but, apart from Earth, nowhere else. Or have they? And what do we mean by 'people'? There is growing evidence that the universe is full of planets orbiting other suns. And where there are planets there might be people.

WHEN WE WALK MINDFULLY DOWN A LANE in the daytime, we are aware of ourselves as surrounded by the living world of nature, the flowers in the hedgerow, the crops in the fields, the birds, the trees and the animals. We might reflect on our relationship with these living things, conscious that we are part of an elaborate web of life that has taken billions of years to evolve into this rich and wonderful complexity on the planet.

But as we walk down a lane at night, when the world around us is in shadow and we stare up at the stars, it is natural to wonder if we are alone in the universe, or if there are other worlds populated by other people. We have discovered that our sun is only one in a universe of a billion suns. Many

of those suns have been found to be accompanied by planets.

The question, which no amount of scientific research has yet been able to answer, is whether life on Earth is unique in the universe, the consequence of a chemical 'accident'; or whether living organisms are a natural development of chemistry and will therefore flourish throughout the cosmos. Which would be the more remarkable – to discover that we are alone in a vast, ancient and dead universe, or to find out that we are only one of a billion living worlds? There is no science at present to guide us and so all we can do is take our own view on the matter.

A Cosmos Full of Observers

I personally believe that life will be found to flourish throughout the cosmos as easily as weeds grow in my garden. The ordinary chemistry of the universe, the oxygen, carbon, nitrogen, iron and so forth, which was created in the first massive stars, is so remarkable that it has within it a principle of self-organization, which naturally leads to life. It has happened here on Earth (quite quickly in cosmic terms) and it will happen elsewhere. The sky may be filled with life on other far-off worlds.

Where there is life there will be evolution, for it follows logically; and where there is evolution, eventually there will be nervous systems and brains. Minds will then emerge, and with minds, mindfulness.

CHAPTER SEVEN

THE PILGRIMAGE

*A pilgrimage is a walk with a goal; its
focus lies in the future. Some, who are religious,
will see it as an act of prayer, a ritual involving the
whole body and not just the mind. For others the goal
will be a secular one: the Jarrow March of unemployed
men trekking down through England to Westminster
in 1936 to advertise their plight; Mahatma Gandhi's
great Salt March to the sea in 1930 to make a
political point; the Aldermaston marchers
demonstrating against nuclear weapons in the
1950s and 60s. They all share something of
the character of a pilgrimage.*

THE HOLY MOUNTAIN: A JOURNEY IN THE SHADOW OF BYZANTIUM

WILLIAM DALRYMPLE

HARPER COLLINS, ISBN 0-00-255509-3

I have been interested for a long time in the relationship between Islam and Christianity, a relationship now sadly being put under great strain by world events, and also by fundamentalist extremism on both sides. Dalrymple walks through the land of origin of both these great faiths. He follows in the footsteps of a 6th-century monk, walking roads that have not been resurfaced since the days of the Romans. The route takes him from the all-male fastness of Mount Athos to the remote monasteries of southern Egypt. He writes beautifully and is as alive to the politics of the region today as he is to the history and theology of the countries he walks through. We are treated to some intriguing speculation about the debt Islam owes to Byzantine Christianity, and discover that St George is revered as a miracle-working saint by Muslims in Syria (if only flag-waving British nationalists knew this!). A theme that saddens him is the devastating decline of Christianity in the land of its birth and in neighbouring countries.

WALKING WITH A GOAL

◆

*Millions have taken to the roads throughout history with a greater
purpose in mind than just the walking. Whether religious or secular,
the eyes of the pilgrim are fixed on the horizon and the 'here and
now' is charged with feelings of anticipation.*

FOR CHAUCER'S CHARACTERS in *The Canterbury Tales*, it was
the shrine of Thomas Becket that drew them; for the
Muslim making the Hajj, whispering 'Lord – here I come,' it
is Mecca. The Hindu may walk the length of the sacred river
Ganges to its source in the Himalayas, even prostrating himself at every step as an additional austerity.

Pilgrimage to a Meteor Crater

I made a secular pilgrimage myself not many years ago with a
special walk in mind. It was in the spring and I flew to Phoe-
nix, Arizona and rented a car for nine days.

There was a lot to see in a richly interesting landscape,
enough to distract me from my goal – the giant cacti with
their own specially adapted species of gila woodpecker, and
the extraordinary wind-sculpted rock pinnacles in the
Chirichahua range of mountains, standing among the pine
trees like tall gothic minarets. The hummingbirds of Millers
Canyon held my attention for hours on end, and a long ribbon
of cottonwood trees by the San Pedro River, corridor for

migrating birds, threatened to divert me for good from my intended quest. Then there were the other attractions of the desert – the unbelievably bold colours of the Painted Desert, and the enormous trunks in the Petrified Forest, fallen trees, with knots, grain and bark intact but turned to stone, lying at all angles on the surface as though abandoned by time. Ancient Indian petroglyphs (small figures carved into the rock) in the desert and the 14th-century rock dwellings of the Sinaguan people near Sedona – they all deserved a trip to Arizona for their own sake. I saw all these wonderful things, but only briefly.

My true goal, my personal pilgrimage, was to a fifty-thousand-year-old feature of the landscape in the north of Arizona near Flagstaff: a meteor crater.

I wanted to walk round its rim.

Memories of the Moon

I had known about the Arizona meteor crater since I was at school. In my teens I built a Newtonian telescope and used it principally for mapping small areas of the moon, its mountains, valleys, craters and all the rubble of the ancient lunar surface. Amateur astronomers could do that usefully in the late 1950s and actually make discoveries. The Apollo missions to land on the moon were not yet even a dream. It was a truly thrilling era.

Astronomers had come round to the view, by then, that the

heavy lunar cratering was not volcanic but due to the impact of meteorites, comets and asteroids. Even a pair of binoculars will reveal the pockmarks of this heavy bombardment, made in the early days of the solar system. Large craters such as Copernicus or Tycho (big enough to house major cities) are visible to the naked eye; and the dark patches called 'seas', which give us the face of the Man in the Moon, are major impact basins where giant asteroids collided with and melted the lunar surface. They are now waterless deserts.

The same celestial bombardment afflicted the Earth but most of the evidence has been worn away by the movement of the planet's crustal plates, by ice ages, wind and rain. The Arizona meteor crater, however, is very new, despite its age compared to human history, and it retains its original features. To walk round its rim would be like walking on the moon – which is why, for such a long time, I had wanted to make this pilgrimage.

Reaching My Goal

I drove along the old Route 66 and stayed at Holbrook in a cheap motel where the nylon bed sheets sparked electric storms in the night – but a pair of mountain bluebirds in the car park the next morning made up for any discomfort!

Although it was late spring there was still snow on some of the pine trees. I drove out to the crater and found myself, blissfully, the only visitor. A sprinkling of snow lay around the

rim. A 150-metre deep hole confronted me, site of a massive explosion bigger than any bomb detonated by man. The crater was smoothly curved at the bottom, then the sides sloped up to rugged walls where strata of sandstone were visible. It was exactly like the smaller craters on the moon that I had drawn and mapped.

I might have been on the moon itself, except the sky was blue instead of black, and here in this crater small pine trees and juniper bushes had rooted around the inner rim. The snow was a giveaway too, and also four magnificent ravens that took flight from the bottom of the crater, circling and gambolling together up into the sky. If rocks had voice, they would croak like those ravens.

The Power of Nature

I was very aware of the transitory and vulnerable nature of my own existence as I picked my way around the rocks of the rim. I stopped to gaze down into that crater, and sat on a rock to take in the dramatic scene. The power of nature confronted me once again. Our newspapers in recent years have been full of pictures of tsunamis, earthquakes and appalling floods. People in their hundreds of thousands have been wiped away without notice. It has always been thus. Nature is haphazard and unthinking in its killing.

In the early history of the Earth there were even greater disasters, many of them caused by asteroids and comets

colliding with the planet, making craters just like the one on whose rim I was now mindfully sitting. The era of the dinosaurs came to an end with one such catastrophe.

It has been argued that we owe our very existence to the mega-disaster that wiped out the dinosaurs. It cleared the ground for the rapid evolution of mammals and hence, from one branch of the primates, of mankind. Some religious people object to this thought on the basis that it undermines our special creation, and that seeing us as an accidental development of evolution robs us of any sense of purpose. It takes away our God-given dignity.

Creative Accidents

But even artists talk about the important role of accidents in their painting or sculpture; if they can, then why not God even more so? We live daily with the unexpected 'haps' of chance. If my father had not impulsively jumped off a bus one day 75 years ago for a swift pint of beer, he might never have met my mother, they might never have married, and I wouldn't be here sitting on the rim of this crater reflecting on the delicate contingency of my life. Does the accidental element in my history make me lose any sense of personal significance? No, not to my mind at all.

After walking the rim, I strolled out into the desert to get a distant view. With any luck I might find some bits of meteorite scattered over the desert. My search for pieces of meteorite was interrupted by the sound of a siren and a police car bounced into view along the track. I had no idea where it came from. A burly policeman with a gun on his hip got out and swaggered towards me. The owners of the land, he informed me, did not care for meteorite-hunters.

I waved my binoculars and bored him to death with a long story of how I had been reliably informed that this was a great place to observe that strange American cuckoo, the roadrunner. Thank heavens he never searched my pockets.

A WALK ON EASTER ISLAND
& THOUGHTS ON HUMAN DIGNITY

◆

Confronted by the Arizona meteor crater and other demonstrations of the awe-inspiring power of nature, we can feel very small, our lives fragile and transitory. It seems that each of us is no more than a blink in the evolutionary process, a single snapshot from aeons of unrolling time.

TRAVELLING AROUND THE WORLD a few years ago, I very much wanted to see the great carved heads of Easter Island. All the pictures I had seen suggested there was something timeless, almost godlike about them. Shrouded in mystery and far from being transitory they seemed to offer hope that there is something immortal about the human form.

THE PILGRIMAGE

SKY BURIAL

XINRAN

DOUBLEDAY, ISBN 0-385-51348-0

Xinran is well known to readers of the *Guardian*, for her regular, much admired column. In *Sky Burial* she retells the extraordinary story of Shu Wen. It is unlike any other, and I found it deeply moving. Shu Wen spent 30 years in Tibet, first with the militia and then with nomads, on a lonely personal quest. Her husband, a doctor, had been transferred to Tibet with the Chinese army in the 1950s. It was only months after their marriage. Shu Wen soon learnt of his death but was given no details. The authorities were more concerned with the relationship between China and Tibet than with her private grief. Her journey across the high plateau of Tibet, to find out how her husband had died, is a tale of loyalty and love: a search through silent mountains for rumours of him; patiently waiting, on one occasion, for a year for snow to clear so that she could trek through a high pass. Her odyssey gives me a different and humbling perspective on all my walking.

I managed to find a flight from New Zealand to Tahiti. From there I could fly to Santiago in Chile, changing planes at Easter Island. This arrangement gave me a week to explore the island on foot.

It is a very friendly place; local people cluster at the airport to offer hospitality for not many dollars.

I was surprised at how *many* heads, carved from the local volcanic basalt, some twenty feet tall, are scattered about the island. There are hundreds. And they are every bit as mysterious as I had imagined, long aloof faces tilted at various angles but always gazing at the far horizon, and usually facing inland. Were they gods or men?

Pilgrimage to the Quarry

I decided to make an 12-mile pilgrimage from one end of the island, where I was staying, to the other, where I would find the quarry from which the rock for the statues had been cut. Easter Island is roughly triangular, with an old extinct volcanic cone at each corner. The quarry was in the flanks of one of these low volcanic hills, Rano Raraku.

The walking was interesting and rather like being on Orkney, except there are very few birds (too far from the mainland for gulls), no planes cross the sky, and the ocean is quite empty of ships. Only the sounds of wind and waves break the silence — and the crunch of my own boots. It is a lonely place, with a small population and one football pitch (fortunately there are two teams living on the island, because the next nearest pitch is over two thousand miles away!). The original population of the island were Polynesian adventurers, and Easter Island was probably the last in the Pacific to be occupied, in the 4th century AD or later.

The story of what happened is well known. Many people

in the history of Easter Island a warning parable. The islanders, for whatever reason, became obsessed with carving the giant heads, which they moved into position on wooden rollers. The place was once heavily wooded, but is now rolling grassland. It is said that, unthinkingly, the islanders cut down all the trees for fuel, to clear the land for crops and to provide rollers for the great task of moving the Moai (as the figures are called) to the platforms where they would be erected. Only then did they realize that they had no wood left with which to build ocean-going canoes. They were stranded.

The community went into decline, and later became slaves to Peru. It was almost the end of their culture. But the modern world has come to their rescue.

Gaze of the Ancestors

Planet Earth is an isolated island in space, with limited resources. Will we make the same unthinking mistake as the islanders? There will be no one to come to *our* rescue if we do.

At Rano Raraku dozens of heads still rest in the cliffs, lie in the ground half-carved, or tilt part upright at the sky at odd angles, exactly where they were first sculpted hundreds of years ago. Each figure is a silent, patient presence, like a god waiting to be born from the earth.

I sat alone to eat my picnic and rest on an inner slope of the volcano, and watched some wild horses galloping around the far side of the crater lake. The only sound, apart from the distant clip-clop of the horses' hooves, was the wind rattling the seedpods of stunted yellow lupins. Fourteen giant heads contemplated the view with me; they rested with the mindfulness of rock in the here and now.

I then revised my opinion of the Moai – they are not gods shrouded in mystery at all. They are people. They were carved, I am sure, to represent ancestors and placed to gaze out over the land of their descendents as guardians (which is why so few face the sea). The remarkable stylized design, and the way they stare at the horizon, gives them a very strange enigmatic air of peace and immortality. Somehow the artists, in carving these figures, have captured the immortal dignity of the human being.

A PILGRIM'S PROGRESS TO HEAVEN OR HELL

Religions have tended to offer their followers rewards for leading a good life ('pie in the sky when you die') and severe punishment for the backslider: the stick and carrot approach. Life is then seen as a pilgrim's progress – hopefully to heaven.

NAIVE PICTURES OF HELL can be vastly amusing – and colourful. The blue frog-like monster devouring naked sinners who tumble down through scarlet flames in the stained-glass windows of Fairford church in Gloucestershire can easily be matched by Buddhist cave paintings of the torments of the damned. In fact, Buddhist scenes of hell are much older than their Christian counterparts – and equally painful to contemplate.

The heavens, too, make for great pictures. The Christian Bible ends with the vision of a New Jerusalem, all gold and jewels – a place of eternal light and no more tears. The colours lend themselves to many a stained-glass window. These visions of heaven have great spiritual value, but for many of us today they are parables or metaphors for the experiences of the inner life. They do not refer to places we might go to after death. There was a time when it seemed obvious to Christian people that a pilgrim's life led to heaven after death. I am not sure that we all think that way anymore.

Walking Without Answers

It has been said that we are always walking towards our own death. It sounds morbid but I don't think so. Our walking will always be in the present moment where happiness and fulfilment are to be found; living in the 'Now'.

I have described earlier how we buried my father in the churchyard in Eskdale. When the service was over, we immediately made our way down the valley to the George the Fourth pub and did what he had asked us to do – we drank a toast, in whisky, to his continued existence. Whenever I am in

the district I make a pilgrimage to that same pub and repeat the toast lovingly.

My own personal conviction is that our short lives on Earth are grounded in an eternal God who loves us. In that, I believe, lies our eternity. We *belong* both before and after death. And our loved ones who are dead have not 'gone' anywhere, for they too belong, and always will. What we will know about life and love, after our own physical death, I have no idea and cannot begin to imagine; and whether it is a state of being in which we have knowledge and awareness or not, I do not know; but I do think it is a matter that can happily take care of itself. And I am content to make the pilgrimage to the pub without answers.

A SHORT FINAL WALK

I want to recount a last walk in this book, which takes us back to Cumbria, where we began, and to another Saxon cross. The goal of this walk, this mini pilgrimage, is St Paul's Church, Irton, which sits on a low rise of land at the foot of Wasdale and Mitredale.

WHEN I WAS WALKING IN AUSTRALIA I found the work of artists helped me understand, and look more effectively at, the landscape. The Aboriginal artist Rover Thomas alerted my eyes to the incredible colours of the

Australian soil. He was born by the thirty-third well on the Canning Stock Route, located near the border of the Great Sandy and Gibson Deserts. Most of his life was spent in the Kimberley region of Western Australia; his deep affinity with the land reveals itself in his paintings of simple shapes and dots. Ancestral events and dreams inspired him.

It was the earth colours, which he ground and mixed for himself, that struck me – dark chocolate and white, cream, ochre and orange, rich terracotta, red and liver purple. They made me look at the land again.

But now I am on a spring walk in Cumbria and the hedgerows and wayside banks are rich in flowers, delicate white wood sorrel, fat bunches of primroses and violets. The hawthorn and hazelnut bushes are still only in bud. The Victorian Pre-Raphaelite artists come to mind and make me look again: Edward Burne-Jones in particular. Pre-Raphaelite painters and stained-glass-window designers made a feature of flowers, placing their elegant and beautifully robed figures, barefooted, in abundant meadows.

The windows in the Irton church that I am visiting on this walk were designed by Burne-Jones and made by William Morris & Co. I had not seen them before.

A Saxon Cross Covered in Plant Patterns
The walk from Gosforth follows a winding road at first, past sycamore trees and over two bridges. The streams (locally

known as becks) are full of water after heavy rain; they rush and gurgle over grey-blue stones, crystal clear and cold. Trees are still bare but waiting to burst into leaf. Lambs gambol in fields where the first dandelions burst yellow in the sun.

The road passes a farm with a sad story to tell. It is called Sorrow Stones. Further along it runs by a sloping field called Hanging How. Just names on a map normally, but today I find them very moving. In previous centuries, anyone convicted of crime and due for hanging – a boy caught for stealing a sheep, perhaps, to feed his family – was allowed a pause and a last pint of ale at Sorrow Stones before being taken up the hill to be hanged. What numbers of wives, mothers, girlfriends, children must have gathered in that sorrowful place over time? I am overwhelmed by thoughts of their sadness and despair as I walk on to the church; I find it hard to shake off. The human condition can be tragic.

I find myself wondering if this is why the cross has become such a riveting symbol for so many people: that somehow Jesus' life and death were marked by both dignity and sorrow, which are both such strong features of human experience.

My Spirits Rise

The path plunges down through some woods and over another stream where some wild daffodils on their short stems stir in the breeze. They are so much more beautiful, I reflect, than the larger cultivated varieties.

I get to the church and the windows do not disappoint, although the flowers at the foot of the figures are all worked in blue; and one of those figures is rather unexpected – a pagan prophetess, the Tiburtine Sybil. Apparently she had predicted the overthrow of all the foes of Christianity (such un-Christian tribal sentiments!) and so earned her place in the stained glass.

The early 9th-century Saxon sandstone cross, dating from before the Danish and Norman invasions, is very different from the one we visited in Gosforth churchyard. There are no figures carved on it, either human or animal. All four sides are covered with organic patterns, plant life turned into geometry; entwined vines and close interlacing rosettes of Irish origin. There is something very pleasing about this artistic statement from over a thousand years ago.

There are hints here, for me, of our place in creation; we are part of an interconnecting and interdependent web of life on Earth. Truth, in the opinion of those who sculpted the cross, lies deeper than words and pictures of people. I find, in this moment of contemplation, my spirits rising again.

It has been a good walk and the hills are catching the afternoon sun, glowing richly in the russet and chestnut colours of last year's bracken.

I think I shall continue the walk another three miles to the George the Fourth pub at the foot of Eskdale for a pint. And, of course, a whisky chaser!

INDEX

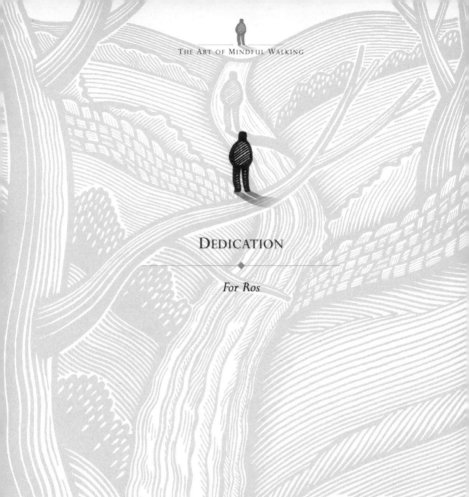

DEDICATION

◆

For Ros